797,885 Books
are available to read at

www.ForgottenBooks.com

Forgotten Books' App
Available for mobile, tablet & eReader

ISBN 978-1-333-81102-0
PIBN 10665275

This book is a reproduction of an important historical work. Forgotten Books uses state-of-the-art technology to digitally reconstruct the work, preserving the original format whilst repairing imperfections present in the aged copy. In rare cases, an imperfection in the original, such as a blemish or missing page, may be replicated in our edition. We do, however, repair the vast majority of imperfections successfully; any imperfections that remain are intentionally left to preserve the state of such historical works.

Forgotten Books is a registered trademark of FB &c Ltd.
Copyright © 2017 FB &c Ltd.
FB &c Ltd, Dalton House, 60 Windsor Avenue, London, SW19 2RR.
Company number 08720141. Registered in England and Wales.

For support please visit www.forgottenbooks.com

1 MONTH OF FREE READING

at

www.ForgottenBooks.com

By purchasing this book you are eligible for one month membership to ForgottenBooks.com, giving you unlimited access to our entire collection of over 700,000 titles via our web site and mobile apps.

To claim your free month visit: www.forgottenbooks.com/free665275

* Offer is valid for 45 days from date of purchase. Terms and conditions apply.

English
Français
Deutsche
Italiano
Español
Português

www.forgottenbooks.com

Mythology Photography **Fiction**
Fishing Christianity **Art** Cooking
Essays Buddhism Freemasonry
Medicine **Biology** Music **Ancient Egypt** Evolution Carpentry Physics
Dance Geology **Mathematics** Fitness
Shakespeare **Folklore** Yoga Marketing
Confidence Immortality Biographies
Poetry **Psychology** Witchcraft
Electronics Chemistry History **Law**
Accounting **Philosophy** Anthropology
Alchemy Drama Quantum Mechanics
Atheism Sexual Health **Ancient History**
Entrepreneurship Languages Sport
Paleontology Needlework Islam
Metaphysics Investment Archaeology
Parenting Statistics Criminology
Motivational

VOLUME 62
NUMBER 4

WHOLE NO. 291
1948

Psychological Monographs:
General and Applied

Combining the *Applied Psychology Monographs* and the *Archives of Psychology* with the *Psychological Monographs*

HERBERT S. CONRAD, *Editor*

This monograph was originally approved for publication in the *Psychological Monographs* by JOHN F. DASHIELL, *Editor*

The Frequency and Affective Character of Childhood Memories

By
SAMUEL WALDFOGEL
Wayne University

A Dissertation Submitted in Partial Fulfillment of the Requirements for the Degree of Doctor of Philosophy in the University of Michigan

Price $1.00

Published by
THE AMERICAN PSYCHOLOGICAL ASSOCIATION, INC.
1515 MASSACHUSETTS AVE. N.W., WASHINGTON 5, D.C.

COPYRIGHT, 1949, BY THE
AMERICAN PSYCHOLOGICAL ASSOCIATION

ACKNOWLEDGMENTS

THE AUTHOR wishes to express his deepest gratitude to Professor John F. Shepard, whose guidance and assistance in the present study were an invaluable asset. He is also gratefully indebted to Professors Charles H. Griffitts, Martha Guernsey Colby, Willard C. Olson, and George Meyer for their keen interest and helpful criticism. To his wife, Diana, whose constant help and encouragement made the present study possible, he owes a special debt of gratitude.

SAMUEL WALDFOGEL

THE LIBRARY

The Ontario Institute

for Studies in Education

Toronto, Canada

TABLE OF CONTENTS

	Page
I. Introduction	1
II. The Frequency and Affective Character of Childhood Memories	7
III. Individual Differences in Childhood Memories	23
IV. Summary	
V. Appendix	

THE FREQUENCY AND AFFECTIVE CHARACTER OF CHILDHOOD MEMORIES

I. Introduction

PREVIOUS INVESTIGATIONS OF CHILDHOOD MEMORIES

PSYCHOLOGISTS of all persuasions are agreed that an individual's childhood experiences exercise a profound influence upon his later behavior. The psychoanalysts—notably Freud—who were among the first to assert this genetic principle, and who have devoted at least as much effort toward its elaboration as any other single group, have emphasized the unconscious character of this influence. They have insisted that the significant events of a person's childhood are repressed (infantile amnesia) and may be made available only through the use of special techniques like psychoanalysis.[1] Indeed Freud (14, p. 178) has stated that those memories of childhood that can be recalled by adults are for the most part "screen-memories," respectable or innocuous disguises for the unconscious contents that underlie them.

In the face of the abundance of clinical evidence, the fact that repressed childhood experiences may be significant for adult behavior can scarcely be questioned. The clinical evidence, however, cannot be construed as proof of the universality or even the predominance of infantile amnesia. Nor does it preclude the possibility that material, spontaneously and correctly recalled from childhood, may also be significantly related to adult behavior. Unfortunately, facts on these matters are conspicuously absent among the investigations of both clinical and experimental psychology. Considering the recognized importance of childhood for later development, the paucity of systematic research on childhood memories is rather surprising. Approximately thirty empirical studies have appeared in the literature since 1893 when Miles (29), employing a questionnaire, asked his subjects to state their earliest recollection.[2] Moreover, most of these studies have been devoted, not to the entire range of childhood recall, but only to some segment of it.[3]

A number of studies deal exclusively with the earliest recollection. In addition to the investigation of Miles, studies are reported by Blonsky (4), Dudycha and Dudycha (12, 13), Gordon (18), and Potwin (32). A study reported by Heinemann (21) was devoted solely to recollections of the first school year. More extensive but still incomplete were studies conducted by Colegrove (8) and Henri and Henri (24) who employed mailed questionnaires to make inquiries regarding early memories. The questionnaires used in these two studies were not unlike one another, and they asked for such information as the first, second, and third mem-

---

[1] As introduced by Freud (16, pp. 580-582), the term "infantile" in this context is intended to include the first six to eight years of childhood. Freud's position is that infantile amnesia is a consequence of the repression of infantile sexuality which manifests itself during this period.

[2] Miles' study was not primarily directed toward childhood memories. The question regarding the earliest memory was only one of many designed to explore the inner life of the individual.

[3] For a more detailed survey of the literature on childhood memories than will be attempted here, see G. J. Dudycha and M. M. Dudycha (11). These writers have summarized all the work done prior to 1941. At the time of preparation of this manuscript no additional researches had come to the author's attention.

ories and the ages thereof; the earliest recollection of the mother, father, siblings, and relatives; the period at which memories first became consecutive, childhood dreams; etc. Not only were their data regarding childhood memories incomplete, but the technique of the mailed questionnaire employed by these investigators, where in some instances the identity of their correspondents was not even known, quite likely vitiated their results to some degree. Another partial survey of childhood recall was made by Henderson (22), who asked his subjects for one hundred memories, beginning with their earliest and scattered throughout their lifetimes with some attempt at an even distribution. Jersild and Holmes (26) confined themselves to the recall of childhood fears. Means (27) in a somewhat similar study sought after the fears of college women.

Complete surveys of childhood memories were made by Child (7) and Crook and Harden (9) who asked their subjects to report all the memories of the first six years.[4] Their studies, however, disclosed nothing of the character of childhood memories since they merely requested their subjects to record a check for each event that they could recall. A further disadvantage of this method is that it is so readily subject to quantitative falsification. It is such a simple matter for the not too scrupulous subject to insert a few extra checks if he so fancies.

No summary of the research on childhood memories would be complete without reference to the work of Murray et al. (30). In their extensive personality study of fifty-one males of college age an exploration of childhood recollections was included. The subjects were brought individually to the experimenter's office where they were asked to lie on a couch with the experimenter sitting in a chair behind the subject. The subjects were given thirty-five minutes in which to recall their experiences before the age of seven. A verbatim account was kept by the experimenter who went over the memories after the allotted time and asked the subjects to tell whether each was pleasant, indifferent, or unpleasant. The subjects were then asked for their favorite fairy story and any special fantasies or dreams. Following this they were given an extensive questionnaire relating to childhood and dealing with: a. *Family Relations*, b. *School Relations*, c. *Kinds and Distribution of Authority*. Finally they were asked if any new memories had occurred to them since the original interview. This is by all odds the most complete research on childhood memories, but very few of the findings are presented systematically by Murray and his associates, who were primarily interested in formulating a methodology for research and a general theory of personality rather than in a systematic presentation of data. This is unfortunate since, because of the intensiveness of their method, they must have accumulated much valuable data.

All of the aforementioned studies included some reference to individual differences in childhood recollection. Differences were noted in the age of the experience recalled, in its affective character, in the age of earliest recall, and in the total number of experiences recalled. However, only four of the investigators made any attempt to systematically relate these differences to differences in the intellect or character of their subjects and here the findings are meagre indeed. Colegrove (8), whose provocative, but incon-

---

[4] The autobiographical accounts of G. S. Hall (20) and R. Henning (23) might be mentioned in this connection. However, neither of these investigators studied any subjects other than himself.

clusive, results will be referred to again, studied qualitative differences in recall in relation to age, sex, and race. Dudycha and Dudycha (13) correlated the age of the earliest recall with intelligence, finding pratically no relation between the two, although they do note the fact that of 10 subjects reporting memories between the first and second years, eight had intelligence scores which were above the average, and five were in the upper quartile of the group.

Crook and Harden (9) attempted to test the hypothesis that repression of childhood memories is associated with neurotic tendencies by correlating Pressy X-O test scores with the age of earliest recall and with the total number of memories. Using only nineteen subjects they found slight correlations between these measures ($-.37$ with total number of memories and $.52$ with age of first recall), and they concluded:

> The more emotionally stable an individual is, as indicated by a low *Pressy* score, the greater number of memories he retains from the first six years of life and earlier the age from which he retains the first memory.

Child (7) repeated the experiment in order to test this hypothesis, at the same time indicating a number of weaknesses in the assumptions underlying it which Crook and Harden had overlooked. He used many more subjects and additional measures of neurotic tendency, and he found practically no relation between the purported measures of infantile amnesia and the degree of neuroticism. Child also correlated the age of earliest recall with scores on the Otis S-A Test of Mental Ability and unlike Dudycha and Dudycha found a slight correlation (.38) between these measures. The implication is that the more intelligent assign their earliest memory to a later age than the less intelligent. There is little to conclude from these fragmentary and contradictory findings except that there is a need for more intensive research on the subject of individual differences in relation to the recall of childhood experience.

In summary of the previous literature it may be said: first, that there are relatively few studies on childhood memory; second, that in many cases the method of obtaining the data was unreliable; third, that the majority of studies dealt with only some aspect rather than the whole of childhood experience; and fourth, that very little attention has been devoted to the study of individual differences in relation to the recall of childhood events.

AIMS OF THE PRESENT INVESTIGATION

The preceding summary clearly reveals a serious gap in our knowledge regarding childhood memories. It was with the aim of partially bridging this gap that the present study was undertaken. Its purpose in general was twofold: first, to obtain more complete information—quantitative and qualitative—in regard to the recall of childhood experiences; second, to study individual differences in recall, particularly in relation to certain aspects of the personality. Specifically, its aims were as follows:

1. To determine the extent to which college students were able to recall the experiences of their first eight years.[5]

2. To determine the emotion experienced in conjunction with these memories, as well as whether they were pleasant, unpleasant, or neutral in character.

3. To determine if individual differences in the extent of recall were related to certain traits of personality—

---

[5] The present study was restricted to college students. Obviously, individuals of other ages and mental capacities must also be studied before any comprehensive generalizations regarding childhood recall may be made.

intellectual and non-intellectual.

4. To determine if individual differences in the affective character of recall were related to these personality traits.

METHODS OF THE PRESENT INVESTIGATION

The investigator of childhood memories is principally concerned with the authenticity of his data. The recall of experiences from early childhood is particularly susceptible to the omissions, distortions, substitutions, and fabrications that characterize the process of remembering. No method of eliciting the recall of childhood experiences can be completely free from error, but the method employed may increase or decrease it considerably. For example, the use of the mailed questionnaire, as employed in the studies of Colegrove (8) and Henri and Henri(24), where the identity of the respondents was not always known is particularly subject to inaccuracies. By contrast, the method of direct interrogation or personal interview, accompanied wherever possible by checking with witnesses of the original occurrence (relatives, friends, teachers, etc.), is manifestly much less subject to error. Dudycha and Dudycha (12, 13) employed the latter method very successfully in their studies of the first childhood memory of college students. Of the several studies of first memories, theirs was by far the best controlled. Other things being equal, this would appear to be the method of choice in the study of childhood memories; but unfortunately, unless one is dealing with relatively few subjects or restricts himself to relatively few memories, the amount of time consumed makes it practically prohibitive.

Since the present study was undertaken with the purpose of covering all the memories of the first eight years, and since the number of subjects employed was large, it was deemed inexpedient to proceed by personal interview and checking. Instead the subjects were assembled in groups and asked to record their memories in writing. Aside from the time-saving factor, the group method had several other advantages to recommend it. It eliminated the possibility of personal influence through direct or indirect suggestion. Further, it permitted the subjects to remain anonymous, which may have encouraged the disclosure of personal and intimate information that might have been deliberately suppressed had their identity been known. Anonymity was also desirable in connection with the use of the personality inventories that were included in the study.

The subjects were recruited from classes in introductory psychology and were assembled in groups that varied from twenty to forty in size.[6] There were one hundred and twenty-four in all, forty-eight male and seventy-six female. At the first meeting of each group a brief prepared statement was made to the subjects regarding the general nature of their role in the experiment and the importance that attached to securing their complete cooperation.[7] Following this each subject was given a slip of paper on which a number had been marked. The slips were distributed in such an obviously random fashion that subjects could not help but be assured that the experimenter had no knowledge of the number that each subject was being given.

After the distribution of the numbered slips, the subjects were informed that the number was to be their sole method of identification during the experiment, and

---

[6] About two-thirds of the subjects were students at Wayne University; the remainder were enrolled at the University of Michigan.

[7] For the complete statement, see Appendix A.

they were asked to keep a record of it so that it would be readily available for future experimental sessions. They were assured that they would remain anonymous, and that no attempt would be made to identify them. They were next presented with the forms for recording their memories.[8] On this form they were instructed to record all the experiences of which they had any knowledge or recollection up to the time of their eighth birthday.[9] They were further instructed to state as accurately as possible the age of each experience to the nearest year of its occurrence. For example, all events occurring between the ages of four and five were to be marked "four" since the subject was four years old at the time. They were also told to check in the appropriate column on the form if the experience was one that they felt sure that they had recalled spontaneously, if it was one that they had not been able to recall but had been told, or if they were uncertain whether or not they had remembered it.

The period for recording memories lasted eighty-five minutes.[10] At the end of this time the subjects were asked to re-read each memory, consider it carefully, and indicate whether each experience had been very pleasant, pleasant, neutral, unpleasant, or very unpleasant. The five point scale was provided on the form for recording the memories, and it was necessary for the subjects only to check the appropriate description. After this step had been completed, they were asked to indicate in the space provided the emotions that they had experienced at the time of the original incident.

Between thirty-five and forty days later, the same procedure was repeated without any forewarning. The second recall was intended as a check on the first. The subjects were instructed to perform the experiment as though they were doing it for the first time, i.e., to try to recall the events of their early childhood, and not to try to remember what they previously recorded. It was explained that for the purposes of the experiment, it was immaterial whether or not anything that they thought of during the second recall period had been included in the first.

The sole criterion for the inclusion of an item was to be the age of its occurrence, and if it had occurred before the age of eight, it was to be included. Otherwise, the instructions and procedure were exactly the same as at the time of the first recall.

During the interval between the two recall periods, the subjects were given a series of tests that required three additional experimental sessions. These tests included the Henmou-Nelson Test of Mental Ability (Form A) to measure intelligence, and the Meyer Memory Test to measure memory.[11] Also included were the following tests of personality and attitude: The Thurstone Personality Schedule, the A-S Reaction Study, and The Wisconsin Scale of Conservatism-Radicalism.[12]

---

[8] For a complete description of this form, see Appendix B.
[9] For the detailed instructions, see Appendix C.
[10] This time interval was the maximum that was possible within a two hour time limit for the experimental session. Although some subjects were still writing at the end of this time, many seemed to be waiting for the experimenter to announce that time was up. It is possible that this period was too long for all subjects to sustain their maximum concentration, but at least it permitted them plenty of time to record their memories so that speed of writing did not become too prominent a factor.

[11] An abridged form of this unpublished test, constructed by George Meyer, formerly of the University of Michigan Psychology Department, was employed. For further details, see Appendix D.
[12] W. H. Sheldon and S. S. Stevens (37, pp. 491-498). This scale is not available in commercial

As previously stated, it was felt that when the personality tests were administered, the anonymity of the subjects was desirable. On the other hand, with the tests of intelligence and memory, it was feared that if the identity of the subjects were unknown, they might not be sufficiently motivated to put forth their best effort. Since the subjects were identifying themselves with a number during the experiment, which only they knew, it was decided to present the intelligence and memory tests last in the series and introduce them as a part of a second experiment not related to the first. The subjects were now instructed to use only their names, for purposes of identification. Afterward, when the subjects were requested to recall their childhood experiences for a second time, they were instructed once more to use their numbers. At the end of the second recall period the intelligence and memory tests were returned to the subjects, and they were asked to detach their names and write in their numbers, so that these data might also be included in the childhood memory experiment. Again they were assured that no attempt had been nor would be made to discover their identities. It can be stated that they complied readily with all instructions, and there was no overt evidence of suspicion or resentment on the part of any.

---

form. It was made available to the writer for use in the present investigation through the courtesy of the publishers, Harper and Brothers.

II. THE FREQUENCY AND AFFECTIVE CHARACTER OF CHILDHOOD MEMORIES

TOTAL NUMBER OF MEMORIES

SINCE the subjects had been requested to number the experiences which they had recorded, it would have been a simple enough matter to determine the total number for each subject, if the judgment of each as to what constituted a single experience had been accepted without question. However, it was deemed likely that some subjects might include more than one experience in a single description, while others might divide the account of a single experience into several parts. It was decided, therefore, to carefully scrutinize each list of memories in order to determine to what extent the number of recorded items and the number of single experiences coincided. Each item was examined personally by the investigator, who regarded it as descriptive of a single event if the elements contained within it were characterized by temporal continuity and/or contextual unity.[13] Approximately 3% of the items were reclassified as a result of this inspection, and although the total number of memories for some subjects was slightly altered, the total for the group as a whole was virtually unchanged.

[13] For a fuller description of the criteria for determining a single experience, see Appendix E.

The total number of experiences for both recall periods will be found in Table I. Totals are given separately for experiences definitely remembered; experiences about which there was some doubt; and experiences which could not be remembered but which had been recounted to the subjects. Percentages of the grand total are also included for each of the above categories. The results are given separately for male and female subjects. This practice of treating male and female results separately will be continued throughout.

As Table I indicates, the incidents that were remembered constitute about 90% of the total. It may be noted that while the total number of recounted experiences remained approximately the same during both recall periods, there was a slight decrease in the number of doubtful experiences, and a slight (somewhat larger) increase in the number of remembered items during the second recall period. The tendency seemed to be in the direction of a feeling of greater certainty of recall during the second period. The numerical results suggest that in some instances those experiences checked as doubtful on their first recall would be checked as remembered on their second recall. A check of the items revealed that this was actually the case for a few memo-

TABLE I
TOTAL NUMBER OF EXPERIENCES FOR BOTH RECALL PERIODS

	Remembered Experiences		Doubtful Experiences		Recounted Experiences		Total
	No.	Pct.	No.	Pct.	No.	Pct.	
Male ($N=48$)							
Period—I	1603	89.15	108	6.01	87	4.84	1798
Period—II	1794	92.62	53	2.74	90	4.65	1937
Female ($N=76$)							
Period—I	2622	90.04	140	4.81	150	5.15	2912
Period—II	2822	92.07	101	3.30	142	4.63	3065

ries. Other than these there were practically no changes in classification. Evidently the degree of certainty that the subjects felt was quite constant. It was only among the doubtful items that any appreciable variation occurred. This is what might be expected, since a feeling of uncertainty regarding the recall of an event may vary in degree, and on some occasions even shift to a feeling of certainty. A shift in this direction during the second recall period was probably reinforced by the fact that the subjects had reproduced the doubtful experiences only a few weeks before, which would have tended to give these experiences a greater degree of familiarity during the second recall period.

In comparing the total number of experiences for the two recall periods, it can be seen that there is an increase for both male and female subjects during the second recall. The increment is approximately 8% in the case of the male subjects, while with the female subjects it almost reaches 10%. The reasons for this increase cannot be given categorically, but at least two factors may be tentatively stated as contributing to this result. First, it was found that the subjects almost without exception recorded shorter descriptions of their experiences during the second period. Since less time was spent in writing, more could be spent in cogitating, and this presumably would be conducive to richer associations. Second, it is possible that the first recall period had a sort of "practice" effect insofar as it (as well as any review that might have occurred during the interval between the two periods) may have weakened or broken down mnemonic interferences. If this actually occurred, retreading the path of childhood memories should have proceeded more quickly and with less interruption during the second recall, and thus it would be expected that greater associative inroads should have been made into the past.

TABLE II

MEAN, STANDARD DEVIATION, AND RANGE OF RECALL SCORES

	Mean	S.D.	Range
Male ($N=48$)			
Period—I	33.40	13.10	5–62
Period—II	37.38	17.08	10–101
Female ($N=76$)			
Period—I	34.50	15.38	9–100
Period—II	37.13	14.47	10–83

In Table II the mean, standard deviation, and range of the number of remembered experiences are given for both male and female subjects. Since the remembered experiences comprise the large majority of the total, and since this study is concerned primarily with events that can actually be recalled from childhood, the analysis and discussion of data will be devoted mainly to this group of experiences. These experiences are referred to as *recall scores* for the sake of convenience in discussing them.

An inspection of Table II directly reveals two facts which bear consideration. First, it is found that the average number of memories for male and female subjects is almost identical during both recall periods. There is some divergence of the S.D.'s, but it is not substantial and is a result of a few scores at the extremes rather than any general difference in the variability of the two groups. Second, it is observed that there is considerable variation of recall within the two groups. In short, while there apparently are marked individual differences in the ability to recall childhood events, these differences do not appear to be related to the sex of an individual.

TABLE III
RELIABILITY COEFFICIENTS OF RECALL SCORES

	r	P.E.$_r$
Male	.70	.048
Female	.76	.032

It is necessary to know something of the reliability of the recall scores before any significance may be attached to the differences that were found among them, a matter which other investigators who obtained such scores have entirely neglected to consider.[14] Reliability was measured by correlating the scores of the first recall period with those of the second. The coefficients of correlations (reliability coefficients) are presented in Table III.

While the magnitude of these coefficients is not great enough for accurate individual prediction, it is large enough in both cases to indicate appreciable individual consistency in the number of memories reported. These results warrant the conclusion that individual differences in the ability to recall childhood events are not purely of a haphazard nature, some persons apparently being able to consistently recall more of their childhood experiences than others.

It was considered important to know not only the degree of consistency from one recall period to the next, but also the degree of identity. This information could be obtained only by carefully comparing, one by one, the memories of the first recall period with those of the second.[15] The results of this comparison are contained in Table IV which includes the mean recall score of the second period together with the mean number and mean percent of new memories, i.e., those appearing for the first time during the second period.

It can be seen in the above table that approximately one half of the memories recorded during the second recall period had not appeared previously. The large number of new experiences indicates that

TABLE IV
INCIDENCE OF NEW MEMORIES DURING THE SECOND RECALL PERIOD

	Mean Recall Score for Period II	Mean Number of New Memories	Mean Percent of New Memories
Male	37.38	17.74	47.45
Female	37.13	18.55	49.95

the availability of specific childhood memories varies considerably from one occasion to another, even when the external circumstances are remarkably similar, and when the two occasions are separated only by a few weeks. That so many new memories should appear, when presumably the conscious *Aufgabe* of the subjects was the same (if the instructions were followed) on both occasions, is a striking manifestation of the subliminal selective character of the mnemonic process recognized by most modern theoretical psychologists.[16] Moreover it suggests that the store of memories was not ex-

---

[14] Child (7), and Crook and Harden (9) correlated such scores with scores on various psychological tests without making any attempt to determine the reliability of the recall scores, despite the fact that they used the highly dubious method of simply having their subjects record a check for each event that they could recall.

[15] This was a most laborious and time consuming task, and its burden was eased only by the fact that, with the exception of a very few cases, there was no doubt regarding the identity of two descriptions of the same experience. The similarity between descriptions may be regarded as support for their authenticity.

[16] For an excellent account of the contributions of theoretical psychology in regard to the selective aspects of memory, see D. Rapaport (33, pp. 114-137).

hausted, even during both periods. It is quite conceivable that additional memories might have been unveiled, had additional opportunities for recall been made available. This refers only to accessible memories, and not to those which would be regarded by the psychoanalyst as being repressed or unconscious.[17]

At first glance, the variability of the memories might appear to challenge the previous conclusion, based on the reliability coefficients, that some individuals are able to recall more of their childhood experiences than others. The conclusion, however, remains valid if it can be demonstrated that the individuals with larger initial recall scores tend to recall more new experiences than those with smaller initial scores. The implication would then be that they have a larger reservoir of memories from which to draw. This possibility was tested by correlating the initial scores with the number of new memories of the second recall period. The coefficients obtained were .36 for the males and .40 for the females. While these coefficients are small, they are in the direction anticipated by the reliability coefficients, and they support the original conclusion. It follows further that a combined recall score based on both recall periods should be more reliable than either of the individual scores. Combined scores were obtained simply by adding the number of new memories of the second period to the first recall score. The combined score represents the total number of unique events that each subject

---

[17] It is recognized that psychoanalysts consider repression as a variable process that permits unconscious material to shift occasionally to the preconscious and may be recalled. However, they regard some memories as being so firmly imbedded in the *unconscious* that they cannot be recalled except through the application of special techniques such as psychoanalysis and hypnosis. See S. Freud (15).

TABLE V
MEAN, STANDARD DEVIATION, AND RANGE OF COMBINED RECALL SCORES

	Mean	S.D.	Range
Male	51.15	20.75	10-114
Female	53.05	22.46	12-137

was able to recall. The mean, standard deviation, and range of the combined recall scores are given in Table V. The combined results emphasize again the essential similarity between the sexes in the extent of recall, and mark the individual differences even more clearly, since the range of scores is extended.

AGE OF RECALLED EXPERIENCES

It will be remembered that earlier in this paper it was stated that the subjects were asked to approximate the age—to the nearest year—at which each incident occurred. Behind this instruction was the recognition that only a rough approximation could be hoped for, but it was felt that even an approximate age for each experience might indicate significant age trends. The actual results—their tenuous nature granted—was quite revealing in this respect. The total and average number of memories appearing at each age, are included in Table VI. Since these data were derived from the combined recall scores, every unique memory recorded during both recall periods is represented. For those memories that were repeated, the age assigned them at the first recall was entered in the compilation of results.

The most notable feature of this table is the steady progression upward with age. Relatively few experiences are recalled before the third year. This is consistent with the investigations of the first childhood recollection, which are in agreement in placing the average age of

TABLE VI
Total and Average Number of Memories Recorded for Each Age

Age	Male		Female	
	Total	Average	Total	Average
Below 1	0	0	1	0.01
1–2	3	0.06	12	0.16
2–3	24	0.50	63	0.83
–4	88	1.83	264	3.47
5	318	6.63	526	6.92
–6	557	11.60	848	11.16
6–7	689	14.35	1051	13.83
7–8	776	16.17	1267	16.67

first recall between the third and fourth year. Further, these studies indicate that the average age of first recall for females is slightly lower than for males, which is also in conformity with the results above.[18] This conformity may be regarded as support for the reliability of the above data. A further check on reliability was made by determining the extent of correspondence between the ages given at the first recall and the ages given at the second recall for those memories that were repeated. This was accomplished by calculating the coefficient of contingency, or C, for the two series of ages. For males C was .79 and for females C was .73. These coefficients indicate an

appreciable degree of consistency from one report to the next. The age assigned to a memory is not, then, merely a chance matter. In this case consistency does not necessarily establish the authenticity of the ages. It is quite possible that the subjects were consistently wrong in reporting ages, but it is also conceivable that they were consistently correct. At any rate consistency is a *sine qua non*. Had there been no consistency from one report to the next, the age data would have been valueless.

Practically all investigators of childhood memories have noted the infrequency with which experiences prior to the third year are recalled, but to the writer's knowledge Table 6 contains the first published data which show the increment of recollection during the succeeding years of childhood. A careful scrutiny of these data discloses certain facts that warrant more than cursory consideration.

It has already been observed that there is an uninterrupted increase in the extent of recall with age. It may be further obobserved that the rate of increase is not constant but increases with each succeeding year up to the age of five and then diminishes. This pattern of first positive and then negative acceleration yields, when plotted graphically, an ogive which

---

[18] Dudycha and Dudycha (13), who carefully authenticated the age of their subjects' first recollection, found that the average age was 3.67 for adolescent males and 3.50 for adolescent females. This corresponds quite closely to the results of other investigators, especially Gordon (18), who obtained average ages of 3.64 for males and 3.40 for females.
In the present experiment the available data did not permit the computation of a precise average because the subjects were asked to indicate age only to the nearest year; and further they were not instructed to indicate which of their recollections was the first. Nevertheless, a rough measure of average age of first recall was computed by averaging the ages at which memories first appeared for each subject, on the assumption that the memories were fairly evenly distributed for each year. This method yielded average ages of 3.64 for the males and 3.23 for the females, which parallel the preceding results quite strikingly.

is illustrated in Figure 1 for both male and female subjects. Since some investigators, notably Thurstone and Ackerson (40), believe that the curve of mental growth is also an ogive, a direct and positive relation between mental growth and the extent of recall is immediately suggested. Not all authorities, it is true, agree that the curve of mental growth is an ogive, and Goodenough (17) goes so far as to state that no single curve adequately represents the growth of intelligence, since the curve obtained depends upon the nature of the tasks set to measure growth. Nevertheless, all agree that the most rapid rate of mental growth is during the early years, diminishing as the individual grows older. Since the ability to organize and retain experiences is a function of intelligence, it is logical to expect the number of memories of any period to vary somewhat with the level of mental development at that period. This expectation is definitely realized in the above results.

The traditional psychological explanations of the fragmentary nature of childhood recollections have emphasized factors directly related to mental development.[19] These explanations have attributed the almost complete amnesia of the very early years to such factors as the inability of the infant to verbalize, his lack of consciousness of self, his inability to adequately conceptualize time, and the lack of development of mnemonic ca-

---

[19] For an able presentation of some of the main attempts to account for the impermanence of early memories, see G. W. Allport (2, pp. 160-161).

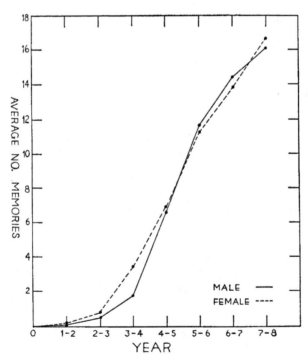

FIGURE 1. Average number of memories for each year (male and female subjects separately).

pacities. As these conditions are altered with the growth and expansion of intelligence, the extent of recollection is presumed to increase. The fact that impressions of a later age are also less distant in time reinforces this tendency.

A comparison of the level of development of the various functions listed above with the extent of recall for any given age should constitute a partial check of the above hypotheses. Data are available to make such a comparison with but two of the functions, namely, memory, and language development. The comparison is graphically presented in Figure 2 which contains curves for (1) the number of childhood memories, (2) the size of children's vocabularies at various ages, and (3) the growth of memory during childhood. The curve showing the number of childhood memories was obtained by combining the results of both male and female subjects of this study. The vocabulary curve was derived from the study by Smith (38) on language development. The memory curve was obtained from the study by Winch (41) in which he employed Stern's *Aussage* test. Stern's test is peculiarly suited to measure the type of mnemonic function involved in the recall of past events since it presents the subject with a complex and meaningful stimulus which he is later asked to describe verbally. In his study Winch

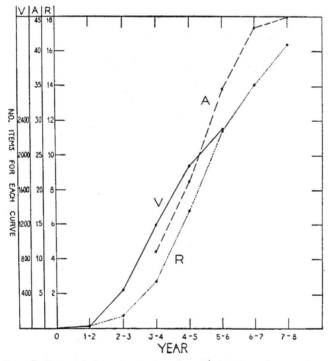

FIGURE 2. Curve R ($N = 124$) shows the number of recollections for each age as determined in the present study. Curve A ($N = 90$) represents the average number of correct items reported on the *Aussage* test for each age. No subjects younger than three years were included. Curve V ($N = 273$) represents the size of vocabulary development at each age. The mid-year level of verbal development was selected in each case. No subjects over six years were included in the vocabulary study.

asked for a report from his subjects both immediately and one week after presentation. The results on both occasions were very similar as far as increase with age was concerned; therefore only the results of the second report have been included.

It can be seen that the curve for memory and vocabulary are also ogives. Moreover, their rate of progression quite closely parallels that of the recollection curve. This is particularly true of the memory (Aussage) curve of which the inflection point is exactly at the same age (5-6) as on the curve of recollection. While this parallel progression cannot constitute final proof that the number of memories which may be recalled from any childhood period is directly related to the level of verbal and memory development of that period, it does bolster the likelihood of such a relation. By way of caution, it should be emphasized that the similarity of the three curves is only relative, all three displaying a similar *rate of increase*. However, there is no way of determining the extent to which the units employed for the curves are comparable to one another. If this could be ascertained, it could conceivably nullify the apparent relationship. Further, it should be noted that the comparisons are solely in terms of averages. Again, if it were possible to make individual comparisons, the ostensive similarity might disappear.

IMPLICATIONS FOR THE DOCTRINE OF INFANTILE AMNESIA

If the foregoing data on the incidence of childhood memories for each age have any validity, they bear directly on the doctrine of infantile amnesia as propounded by Freud. According to this doctrine, the experiences of the first six to eight years are cloaked by a curtain of repression and become available only through free association and dream interpretation. At best a few memories may be recalled, but these are usually banal in content, and their function presumably is to disguise vitally significant experiences that have been repressed (screen-memories). Freud's writings on this subject are quite explicit. In discussing the repressive factors in infantile amnesia, he states (16, pp. 581-582):

> I refer to the peculiar amnesia which veils from most people (not from all) the first years of their childhood, usually the first six or eight years. So far, it has not occurred to us that this amnesia should surprise us, though we have good reasons for it. For we are informed that during those years which have left nothing except a few incomprehensible memory fragments, we have vividly reacted to impressions, that we have manifested human pain and pleasure and that we have expressed love, jealousy and other passions as they then affected us. . . .
>
> On the other hand we must assume, or we may convince ourselves through psychological observations on others, that the very impressions which we have forgotten have nevertheless left the deepest traces in our psychic life, and acted as determinants for our whole future development. We conclude therefore that we do not deal with a real forgetting of infantile impressions but rather with an amnesia similar to that observed in neurotics for later experiences, the nature of which consists in their being kept away from consciousness (repression).

This quotation leaves no doubt in the reader's mind as to Freud's opinions on the matter of childhood recollections; the picture he portrays is quite clear. From it one expects that no one but the exceptional individual will retain more than a "few incomprehensible memory fragments" from the first six to eight years of his life. This contention is rather sharply contradicted by the results of the present investigation which demonstrate that the average college student is able to recall some fifty memories from this early period, and under conditions which were not the most ideal for eliciting recall.[20] Furthermore, the results of this experiment show that the number of memories increases with each successive year in a manner parallel to the development of mental functions. How can the Freudian explain this increase with age? If the forgetting of childhood events is primarily a result of repression, the implication would be that either the repressive forces relax as the child grows older or that his conflicts become less severe. Neither of these explanations is consistent with Freudian theory which asserts: first, that the superego, the *raison d'etre* for repression, does not fully develop until the fifth or sixth year; and second, that the Oedipus complex, the source of the most intense conflict and anxiety of childhood reaches its most acute phase at about the same age.[21]

AFFECTIVE CHARACTERISTICS OF THE RECALLED EXPERIENCES

The psychoanalyst might protest that there is no evidence that the memories elicited in this study were not screen-memories; that although an average of fifty might be a larger number than would have been anticipated by reading Freud, the theory of infantile amnesia remains intact if only banal distortions of really vital childhood experiences are retained by the adult. In commenting on the nature of screen-memories, Freud (14, p. 178) states:

> Memory deals with a mass of impressions received in later life by a process of selection, retaining what is important and omitting what is not; but with the recollections retained from childhood this is not so. They do not necessarily reflect important experiences in childhood, not even such as must have seemed important from the child's standpoint, but are often so banal and meaningless in themselves that we can only ask ourselves in amazement why just this particular detail has escaped oblivion. I have tried with the help of analysis to attack the problem of childhood amnesia and of fragments of recollection which break through it, and have come to the conclusion that, whatever may appear to the contrary, the child no less than the adult only retains in memory what is important; but that what is important is represented (by the processes of condensation and, more especially, of displacement, already familiar to you) in the memory by something apparently trivial. For this reason I have called these childhood recollections *screen-memories*; a thorough analysis can evolve from them all that has been forgotten.

From Freud's description of childhood memories one is led to believe that they are, for the most part, meaningless and trivial distortions of the events of childhood. A perusal of the memories themselves, however, discloses that apparently just the opposite is true. Indeed the memories seemed genuinely to express the "human pain and pleasure, . . . love, jealousy, and other passions" which Freud rightly regarded as belonging to childhood experience.[22] Through them

---

[20] The objection might be raised that even fifty memories constitute only a small fraction of the total number of childhood events. While this is true, it still seems like a considerable number when one remembers that the subjects were limited to eighty-five minutes on each occasion. There is also the fact to consider that the impersonal classroom atmosphere is probably less effective in stimulating recall than an intimate interview situation. Then too, it must be remembered that the period from which the experiences were recalled was considerably removed in time allowing ample opportunity for "normal forgetting." It would be valuable to have a record of the memories of the next four or five years for purposes of comparison. If the theory of infantile amnesia is correct a marked increase in the number of memories after the age of eight should be expected. In view of the gradual increase from ages three to seven, a sudden increase beginning at age eight does not seem probable.

[21] Brown (6, pp. 193-208), on the basis of the opinions of a number of psycho-analytic authorities, places the "phallic stage" of development between the ages of three and seven. This is the period of the Oedipus and castration complexes, the period of the "repression of infantile sexuality" during which development of the "superego (is) complete." This coincides exactly with the period during which memories began to appear in appreciable numbers in the present study.

[22] The writer has no intention of disputing the existence of screen-memories. Freud and other analysts have presented convincing examples of such memories together with their analyses. The question is the extent to which such memories

is reflected the panorama of childhood: the adventure and fun, the bewilderment and awe, the disappointment and triumph, the fear and conflict, the love and hate. It is not meant to imply that the memories accurately represent the pattern of psychosexual development that the Freudians contend is normal, but they do include experiences which are typically associated with childhood and "that must have seemed important from the child's standpoint."[23] Included were a few memories of a frankly sexual nature (eight altogether). These dealt chiefly with experiences involving playmates, only one mention being made of masturbation, and none of sexual feelings towards the parents. It is likely that there was a deliberate suppression of sexual and other very intimate experience of which the subjects felt ashamed. Despite the instruction to include all memories and the assurance of anonymity, it would be sanguine to believe that none of the subjects exercised censorship in their disclosures. More frequent than reports of overt sexuality were accounts of sexual infatuations. That such infatuations are quite common during childhood was demonstrated by Bell (3) as long ago as 1902.

Since the recollections dealt with complex experiences of an extremely diverse nature, they could have been classified according to an almost innumerable variety of schemes. The system of classification in Table VII was adopted for the purpose of giving a general idea of the most frequently recurring kinds of experiences. This does not purport to be an exhaustive list of all the possible categories.

In Table VII it is manifest that the memories covered the gamut of childhood experience. Here surely are events that must have been important to the child. The only question that may be raised is in regard to the authenticity of the recollections. What assurance is there that they are not distortions of actual experiences, or that they are fabrications? The answer is that there is no assurance other than the realistic nature of the events reported and the statements of the subjects that they felt certain that they could actually recall these events. Obviously this is not conclusive. Ideally the accuracy of each memory should have been separately checked, but reasons have already been given why this was not feasible. Unquestionably distortions of the original experiences occurred, but if so, were they any greater than would occur for experiences of a later age that were equally remote in time? If not, then there is no reason to suppose that the fundamental structure of most memories was altered, even though certain details may have been inaccurate. No doubt some memories are spurious, but if it is remembered that Dudycha and Dudycha (13) authenticated memories dating back to the third year and earlier, it is not unreasonable to accept the majority of memories as being probably genuine. Perhaps the Freudian would insist that only a complete analysis of each memory would constitute an adequate check, but until it is clinically demonstrated that screen-memories are the rule rather than the exception, the present evidence must be at least tentatively accepted.

---

are typical of childhood recollections. Freud's writings definitely give the impression that they are the rule rather than the exception.

[23] It is not the purpose of this study to consider the validity of the Freudian theory of psychosexual development. Whatever the psychodynamic pattern of development, it does not follow that an individual is able to insightfully comprehend it simply because he is able to correctly recall important experiences from the early years. The issue is recall and not insight. Freud has stated that amnesia exists for the early years. At the very least, results of this study cast some doubt on this assertion.

TABLE VII
Showing the Most Commonly Recalled Experiences

A. Memories of Personal Experiences, Feelings, Attitudes, etc.
   1. Success and accomplishment.
   2. Failure, frustration, and deprivation.
   3. Fear, worry, and guilt.
   4. Embarrassment and humiliation.
   5. Awe, wonder, curiosity, and confusion.
   6. Sexual feelings and erotic attachments.
   7. Favorite possessions: toys, pets, clothes, etc.
   8. Injury and illness.
   9. Dreams and nightmares.*

B. Memories Relating to the Family**
   1. Feelings and attitudes towards members of family.
   2. Familial practices and activities.
   3. Familial conflict: parents and siblings.
   4. Birth of sibling.
   5. Parental discipline and punishment.
   6. Illness, injury, and death of members of family.

C. Memories Relating to the Neighborhood
   1. Friends and neighbors.
   2. Neighborhood play and activity.
   3. Quarrels and fights.
   4. Exciting events: accidents, fires, scandals, etc.
   5. Moving to a new neighborhood.

D. Memories Relating to School and Church
   1. Teachers.
   2. Classmates.
   3. Activities: plays, programs, sports, festivals, etc.
   4. Favorite subjects.
   5. Disciplinary incidents.
   6. Embarrassing incidents.
   7. Promotions and failures.

E. Memories of Recreational Activities
   1. Trips and vacations.
   2. Parties and holidays (including gifts received).
   3. Picnics and outings.
   4. Visits to friends and relatives (also being visited).
   5. Shows, circuses, carnivals, etc.
   6. Special treats.

* Only a few dreams were reported.
** Relatives are included.

No attempt was made to determine the relative incidence of each type of experience listed in Table VII for two reasons. First, in many instances the classification of an item would have been a highly uncertain—and in the last analysis arbitrary—matter since the rubrics overlap. For example, a memory of misbehavior at school for which the child was later disciplined at home could be classified as either a personal, school, or family experience. Second, it was felt that the emotions accompanying an experience were of greater significance than the setting in which it occurred, and that these items could be most meaningfully classified in terms of these emotions.

A classification of the emotions was derived from the emotional terms with which the subjects had characterized their memories. Altogether a total of 476 different emotional terms were used by the subjects, but many of these were similar to one another, describing the same general kind of emotion.[24] From this list a total of twenty-three generic emotional categories were empirically selected as being adequately representative. These categories are listed in Table VIII together with the relative frequency with which each occurred. It should be emphasized that the total number of emotions is not equal to the total number of memories, since some memories were characterized by more than one emotion, and others included no emotional description at all.

Unless the terms employed by the subjects were merely verbal labels retrospectively applied, they indicate a wide variety of emotional experiences. Since emotional differentiation proceeds quite rapidly during childhood and, as Bridges (5) has demonstrated, is quite advanced

---

[24] For the original list of terms and their frequency of occurrence, see Appendix F.

even at two years, it is entirely possible that the variegated feelings and emotions of childhood are accurately reflected in this list. Interestingly, the distribution is again very similar for both male and female subjects—even for emotional experiences where sex differences might most be expected to appear.

The dominant emotion is *joy*, approximately thirty percent of the total, with *fear* next in frequency, approximately fifteen percent. This is not consonant with the findings of Dudycha and Dudycha (12), who, though they dealt exclusively with the first memory, were the only investigators to include a differential emotional analysis in their study. They found that *fear* was dominant, comprising about forty percent of the total with *joy* next, comprising about twenty-four percent. The relative frequencies of the other emotions that they reported, namely: *anger, wonder-awe,* and *sorrow-*

TABLE VIII
RELATIVE FREQUENCY OF EMOTIONS OCCURRING WITH MEMORIES

Emotion	Percent of Total	
	Male	Female
1. Joy, delight, elation.	29.6	30.5
2. Fear, anxiety, worry.	16.1	14.6
3. Pleasure, pleasantness.	9.3	5.8
4. Anger, hate, resentment.	6.8	6.9
5. Grief, sadness, longing.	5.5	7.0
6. Excitement, adventure.	4.7	5.8
7. Awe, fascination, wonder.	4.3	3.0
8. Displeasure, pain.	3.0	3.0
9. Pride, self-esteem.	2.5	4.8
10. Guilt, shame.	1.8	1.5
11. Embarrassment, humiliation.	1.7	1.7
12. Surprise, amazement.	1.7	1.4
13. Affection, love.	1.4	1.0
14. Curiosity, inquisitiveness.	1.4	2.0
15. Frustration, disappointment.	1.3	1.4
16. Contentment, peace.	1.0	0.5
17. Disgust, revulsion.	1.0	1.2
18. Hurt pride, rejection.	1.0	0.6
19. Bewildered, confused.	0.7	0.7
20. Amusement.	0.4	0.4
21. Anticipation, expectancy.	0.4	0.6
22. Envy, jealousy.	0.4	0.5
23. Pity, sympathy.	0.4	0.5
24. Miscellaneous	3.7	4.7

dissapointment, correspond much more closely to the results in Table VIII. Since Dudycha and Dudycha's study dealt only with the first memory, their results are not directly comparable to the present findings; and the differences in the relative frequencies of the emotions may be due to the difference in the sampling of memories.

Other emotions occurring with considerable frequency in the present study were *pleasure, anger, grief*, and *excitement*. The infrequent appearance of curiosity, guilt, and envy was rather surprising. The rare occurrence of *pity* is interesting and might be a reflection of the egocentric personality of the young child.

A comparison of the relative frequencies in Table VIII suggests a predominance of those experiences that might be considered pleasurable over those that could be regarded as disagreeable. The precise extent of predominance was determined from the subjects' own affective judgments. It will be recalled that the subjects were asked to indicate whether their memories were of events that were very pleasant, pleasant, neutral, unpleasant, or very unpleasant. Although a five point scale was used in the experiment, the results indicated that it failed in its purpose to secure greater refinement in measuring the intensity of feeling, and it was contracted to a three point scale for purposes of quantitative study.

A tabulation of the affective judgments is presented in Table IX. Except for the male memories below the age of three the affective pattern of recall is very consistent for both sexes.[25] The predominance of pleasant over unpleasant memories is quite marked. The ratio is approximately five to three. While not all investigators of childhood memories find this predominance, most of them do. Dudycha and Dudycha (11) in summarizing the results of former studies state:

> Thus we find that, as the matter stands now, the reports are better than two to one in favor of the recall of pleasant memories as against unpleasant ones.

There has been much more unanimity regarding the predominance of pleasant over unpleasant memories among the investigators who studied the ability to recall life experiences of a later age. Moreover, these investigators were able to institute a sort of control by comparing immediate recall of events of a preceding period with delayed recall of events for the same period as, for example, in the oft-quoted studies of Meltzer (28) and Jersild (25). In this way they were able to determine that pleasant experiences survived more frequently.

In the present study as in all other studies of childhood memories, it is impossible to know the original incidence of pleasant and unpleasant experiences. Perhaps the predominance of pleasant memories was directly proportional to the incidence of such experiences in childhood. Still, the possibility exists that the present results are a reflection of the same mnemonic pattern which has manifested itself in most of the studies on the recall of life experiences. A pattern, incidentally, which represents only the average trend, and which is reversed for some individuals.[26]

The tendency for the majority of indi-

---

[25] The total number of memories for males below the age of three was only twenty-seven, an average of approximately one-half per subject. Obviously this number was too small to provide an adequate sample.

[26] The differences among individuals in this regard were noted by investigators from the very beginning, and the terms *memory optomist* and *memory pessimist* came into vogue. Similar differences, which will be discussed in the following section, were also observed in the present investigation.

TABLE IX
Percentage Distribution of Affective Judgments*

	P	N	U	P & U	C R	O
Years I & II						
Male	20.0	32.0	24.0	4.0	16.0	4.0
Female	46.8	15.2	26.6	2.5	5.1	3.8
Year III						
Male	44.2	15.8	26.3	7.4	5.3	1.1
Female	46.9	15.1	25.4	5.2	7.0	0.3
Year IV						
Male	47.2	20.8	22.0	6.9	2.2	1.0
Female	47.0	17.9	26.0	5.0	2.7	1.5
Year V						
Male	52.2	19.0	23.2	3.2	1.6	0.7
Female	42.8	20.6	27.4	5.5	2.6	1.0
Year VI						
Male	43.3	18.7	23.2	4.8	2.5	1.5
Female	43.2	18.1	29.1	5.7	3.2	0.8
Year VII						
Male	47.1	13.6	30.6	6.1	1.5	1.0
Female	45.9	16.9	28.3	5.2	2.6	1.0
Total						
Male	47.4	17.0	27.0	5.4	1.8	1.4
Female	44.8	17.5	28.2	5.4	3.0	1.2

* P, N, and U represent *pleasant, neutral,* and *unpleasant* respectively; C R stands for *cannot remember* and O for *omitted*.

viduals to report more pleasant than unpleasant memories was erroneously interpreted by some investigators as corroboration of the Freudian theory of repression.[27] The irrelevancy of such evidence for the Freudian theory of repression has been cogently discussed by both Sears (36) and Rapaport (33, pp. 69-77). They clearly show that by repression Freud was referring to the tendency to *avoid the awakening of pain through memory,* which is not always synonymous with forgetting the disagreeable. For example, many disagreeable ideas might be retained because of the demands of the *reality principle* of which Freud was highly cognizant. Further, pleasant or innocuous ideas might be repressed because of an unconscious association with a prohibited impulse. And, of course, an experience which was originally disagreeable might lose its unpleasant quality and even be pleasant upon recall, as, for example, when we laugh about discomfiture in a previously embarrassing situation. However, regardless of its relevancy to the Freudian theory of repression, this apparent tendency for most people—not all—to remember experiences that they judge as having been pleasant better than those they regard as having been unpleasant appears to be a matter which merits the most careful consideration. Judging from the writings of individuals who have discussed this phenomenon, it

[27] Or as in the case of Wohlgemuth (42), who found an opposite tendency, to erroneously regard it as refutation of this theory.

does not seem that its full import has been recognized. More shall be said on this subject in the next section which deals specifically with individual differences in pleasant and unpleasant memories.

An even more pronounced characteristic of the affective pattern of recall was the relative infrequency of neutral memories. Fewer than one-fifth were described as neutral, and even these did not appear to be neutral in the sense that the subject had been indifferent to the situation recalled or unaffected by it. Apparently these memories were neutral not because there were no feelings, but because the subject seemed unable to consciously interpret his feelings as either pleasant or unpleasant. For example, the following memory reported as dating back to the age of three: "Watching neighbor being taken away in an ambulance." Surely this experience, which was marked neutral, must have been of intense interest to the young child, and surely it must have awakened feelings; yet it is quite conceivable that even a sophisticated observer could not have arbitrarily classified these feelings as either pleasant or unpleasant (these are not the only dimensions of affective experience), and that the subject was quite correct in describing them as neither. Thus, the prevalence of "feeling" memories was, if anything, even greater than the percentages indicate. The preponderance of *affective* over *non-affective* memories is a universal finding among investigators. This is true of childhood as well as for later periods.[28] This suggests that in order to be retained, experiences must be ego-involving or must have personal relevance for the individual, a fact which perhaps has not always been properly appreciated by psychologists.[29]

THE DOUBTFUL AND UNRECALLED EXPERIENCES

The subjects were instructed to record experiences that they could not recall, but which they had heard discussed, as well as those about which they were uncertain. The reason for this was that it was anticipated that there might be considerable numbers of such experiences which would provide an interesting basis for comparison with experiences that could definitely be recalled. Actually, they were much smaller in number than expected (see Table I), and in content they seemed to be little different from the bona fide memories. They were distinguished from the latter chiefly by the fact that they appeared in relatively larger numbers during the early years, which is what would be expected in the light of all that was disclosed about the relation between age and extent of recall.

The relative frequency at each age of the three classes of experience is given in Table X. It shows the percentage of the total number that occurred at each age. For the remembered experiences there is an increment with each year, and approximately sixty percent of the memories are assigned to the ages of six and seven. With the doubtful and recounted experiences, however, the central tendency shifts to below the age of six. Only

---

[28] For a complete summary of the experimental studies on memory in relation to affectivity, see D. Rapaport (33, pp. 41-103).

[29] Concerning this Stern (39, p. 223) writes: "But in reality no *association* can originate in the *individual without having personal relevance*. The person has mnemonic susceptibility for such contiguities in experience as are not inconsequential and indifferent to him."

TABLE X
Percentage Distribution of Experiences for the Various Age Levels

	Remembered Experiences		Doubtful Experiences		Recounted Experiences	
	Male	Female	Male	Female	Male	Female
Below 1	0	0.0	0	0	3.9	2.6
1–2	0.1	0.3	4.2	3.4	5.8	12.2
2–3	1.0	1.6	7.6	10.3	24.2	21.2
3–4	3.6	6.5	17.8	24.0	14.5	20.0
4–5	13.0	13.1	18.6	17.1	19.4	14.8
5–6	22.7	21.0	19.5	13.7	11.6	15.5
6–7	28.1	26.1	16.1	19.8	9.7	5.8
7–8	31.6	31.4	16.1	11.6	10.7	7.8

about thirty percent of the doubtful experiences are dated at six and seven; and of the recounted ones, approximately fifteen percent for females and twenty percent for males are found in this period.

III. INDIVIDUAL DIFFERENCES IN CHILDHOOD MEMORIES

DIFFERENCES IN FREQUENCY OF MEMORIES

ALTHOUGH the results in the preceding section seem to refute the notion that infantile amnesia is practically universal, they do suggest that it occurs with some individuals. At least they demonstrate that differences in the ability to recall childhood events are indeed very great. For males the recall scores ranged from 10-114; while for females the range was from 12-137. Thus, for both sexes the highest score was over eleven times as great as the lowest. It does not seem reasonable that differences of such magnitude could be accounted for solely by differences in the eventfulness of the early lives of the subjects. It does not even seem likely that differences in affective intensity of experience could explain them. One would expect intense experiences to be more evenly distributed in the lives of children, particularly since intensity of experience depends upon subjective as well as objective factors. It is surely no error to assume that all children's lives are rich in subjectively intense experience.

Whatever variations may have occurred in the frequency and intensity of the original experiences there was obviously no way of assaying them. But it was felt that factors of individual selection were probably at least as important in determining differences in the memories. These factors it was presumed could be either intellective or non-intellective (emotional, temperamental, attitudinal) in nature, and, therefore, in measuring individual differences an attempt was made to include both types of traits. The relation between the intellective functions—especially memory—and the ability to recall events of the past is an obvious one. Less obvious, but also regarded as important are the emotional and conative tendencies of the individual. Memory was thus conceived as not simply the "ability to revive accurately impressions once obtained, but as the integration of impressions into the whole personality and their revival according to the needs of the whole personality."[30]

The intellectual traits selected for measurement were general intelligence and memory. Other traits—visual imagery, for example—are probably equally important in the retention of life experiences, but in face of the limitations of time and the method of group administration, these two tests were selected as most practicable and pertinent. Intelligence was measured by the Henmon-Nelson Test of Mental Ability, Form A. The Meyer Memory Test (See Appendix D) was employed to test mnemonic capacity.

The measurement of the non-intellective traits of personality presented a more serious problem. The factors that determine retention of individual experiences must necessarily be highly individual and depend upon a complex balance of forces. In the group situation it is possible to obtain information only on relatively isolated and general traits of personality. Any relationship discovered between such traits and retention of childhood events could not without additional evidence be interpreted as a causal one, but if such a relationship were discovered, it would at least attest to the fact of the relatedness of personality and recall. With the methodological

---

[30] D. Rapaport (33, p. 112).

limitations of this approach in mind, a battery of three tests was selected that would reflect rather separate and diverse facets or dimensions of personality. The Thurstone Personality Schedule was used to measure the area of emotional stability, the A-S Reaction Study to measure a fundamental trait of personality, and the Wisconsin Scale to measure a fundamental attitude.

In order to determine if there was any relationship between the number of childhood memories and the psychological traits measured, a comparison was made of individuals whose recall scores were at the extremes of the distribution. This method of comparison was deemed preferable to the method of correlation because high coefficients were not anticipated in view of the complexity of factors influencing childhood memories, and low correlation coefficients sometimes mask significant relations that exist at the extremes but do not hold for the middle of a distribution.[31] Further, by comparing the extremes with the middle of the distribution, any tendency toward curvilinear relationships could be readily ascertained. Therefore, for purposes of comparison the subjects were divided into quartiles on the basis of their recall scores. Table XI is arranged to permit a direct comparison between subjects with high, average, and low recall scores.

Except in one or two instances there seems to be relatively little variation among the three groups. This is true for both male and female subjects. In no instance was there any appreciable tendency toward a curvilinear relation, so it was decided to test only differences between the extremes for significance. In each case the difference in mean score

---

[31] This was strikingly demonstrated in Dudycha's (10) study on punctuality.

TABLE XI
A Comparison of Test Results of Individuals with
High, Average, and Low Recall Scores

Test	Mean Scores		
	Upper 25%	Middle 50%	Lower 25%
Intelligence			
Male	59.58	57.00	54.42
Female	49.39	51.77	52.65
Memory			
Male	23.50	26.83	26.91
Female	23.67	23.62	24.07
Emotional Stability			
Male	36.55	40.00	46.33
Female	39.21	40.41	47.50
Ascendance-Submission*			
Male	56.08	47.48	51.25
Female	62.05	54.26	47.17
Conservatism-Radicalism**			
Male	57.82	58.05	56.50
Female	49.36	47.69	58.88

* Negative scores were removed by adding fifty to each score.
** A low score is indicative of conservatism.

TABLE XII

SIGNIFICANCE OF THE DIFFERENCES IN TEST RESULTS BETWEEN INDIVIDUALS WITH HIGH AND LOW RECALL SCORES

Test	Difference Between Means	Difference / σ Diff.
Intelligence		
Male	5.16	1.30
Female	3.26	1.03
Memory		
Male	3.41	1.18
Female	0.40	0.23
Emotional Stability		
Male	9.78	1.08
Female	8.29	1.22
Ascendance-Submission		
Male	4.83	0.84
Female	14.88	2.88
Conservatism-Radicalism		
Male	1.32	0.23
Female	9.41	2.38

between the upper and lower quartiles was divided by the standard error of the difference. These results are given below in Table XII.

It is apparent that the differences between the test results of high and low groups do not even approach statistical reliability except in one or two instances. In no case does the critical ratio exceed 3.00, which is generally accepted as the point of genuine significance.

Practically no relation existed between the recall scores and intelligence, or the recall scores and memory ability. There seemed to be a slight tendency for male subjects with higher recall scores to get higher intelligence test scores, but this tendency was reversed for the females, and neither difference was statistically significant. The differences between the groups on the memory test were equally inconclusive. A greater degree of relationship might have been expected between these measures, but apparently for the group studied—which from the point of view of intellectual ability was fairly homogeneous—neither intelligence nor memory ability was a relevant factor in retaining childhood memories. Of course, it must be remembered that the differences in intellectual capacity that existed at the time of the experiment were not necessarily indicative of differences that existed during childhood. Rate of mental growth is a highly variable process, and it is possible that as children the subjects would have been very differently distributed in regard to memory ability and intelligence. After all, it is the level of mental development at the time of the experience and not its ultimate level that would be the determining factor. Still, insofar as the results of the present experiment are concerned, these intellective factors did not seem to be related to the recall of childhood experiences.

The lack of correlation between the intellective variables and the number of childhood memories stands in apparent contradiction to the earlier finding (see page 13) that the number of childhood memories on the average varied with age and was apparently related to mental development. Careful scrutiny of the results will show that this is not the case. The earlier finding that the frequency of childhood memories increases with age implies that a certain level of mental development is necessary for mnemonic fixation and that a higher level of development permits a greater amount of retention. Higher level must be interpreted to mean higher both in degree of mnemonic capacity and in complexity of mental organization. This is quite compatible with the second finding if one assumes that individual differences in intelligence above a certain critical level (all the subjects were above average in intelligence) are less important than other selective factors in determining the extent of childhood recall.

The results on the personality tests were suggestive of a few trends, but no really impressive relations were noted. Both male and female subjects with high recall scores tended to get lower scores on the Thurstone Personality Schedule, indicating a greater degree of emotional stability; however, statistically this tendency was not very significant. It does coincide, however, with a similar slight tendency found by Crook and Harden (9). From this apparent relationship between infantile amnesia and neurotic tendency, they erroneously concluded that they had found corroboration for the Freudian theory of the relation between repression and neurosis. Child (7) has convincingly demonstrated the errors in the assumptions and conclusions of Crook and Harden, and his arguments will not be repeated here. Suffice it to say that although Freud regarded repression as the essential preliminary condition for the development of neurotic symptoms, he also felt that repression of infantile sexuality was a characteristic of normal development. In any case, the results of the present study reveal very little relation between childhood memories and emotional stability.

With the male subjects there is practically no difference between the scores of the high and low groups on either the A-S Reaction Study or The Wisconsin Scale of Conservatism-Radicalism. With the female subjects, on the contrary, those whose recall scores were higher tend to be more conservative and more ascendant. Neither of these tendencies is thoroughly reliable (although the $D/\sigma D$ of the latter approaches the critical point of 3.00), and since neither is confirmed by the male results, an artefact resulting from sampling is a possibility. Without additional supportive evidence, it would be foolhardy to attempt any generalization regarding the meaning of the differences between the female groups. Nevertheless, they are provocative insofar as they suggest a possible relationship between the personality and the frequency of childhood memories.

In summary it may be said that except in one or two instances, no significant relation was found between the number of childhood memories and the various psychological measures employed. In these instances the relationship, *per se*, was not marked, but was regarded as suggestive of the possibility that non-intellective factors in personality play a determining role in the selection of childhood memories. In view of limitations of the questionnaire method of measuring single traits of personality, as compared to the multiplicity of factors that may influence memory and the complex interrelationships that may exist among them, even a slight relationship may be of significance. Finally, it should be remembered that any relation between personality and memory is perhaps more apt to manifest itself in the content rather than the extent of memory.

DIFFERENCES IN AFFECTIVE CHARACTER OF MEMORIES

It has already been noted (see page 20) that with most subjects pleasant memories appeared with greater frequency than unpleasant ones, but that with some this tendency was reversed. To what extent the frequency of pleasant and unpleasant memories for any given individual is a reflection of the relative incidence of such experiences during his childhood could not be known. There is reason to believe that the relative frequency of pleasant and unpleasant experiences may vary considerably among individuals. Therefore, in comparing individuals in regard to the frequency of pleasant and unpleasant memories, there is no way of knowing to what extent these differences are a result of individual variation in the relative frequency of such experiences during childhood, or to what extent they result from individual mnemonic selective factors. Nevertheless, there is value in making an empiric comparison of these differences from the point of view of personality factors to which they may be related; since the affective pattern of a person's childhood memories is a characteristic of his behavior regardless of the factors producing this pattern. At least it is certain that these are the impressions which are sufficiently relevant to have been retained over a long period of time.

Since the total number of memories differed considerably from one subject to another, comparisons in terms of the absolute number of pleasant and unpleasant experiences could give no indication of the relative frequency of these memories. The relative frequency of pleasant and unpleasant memories could be expressed only by a ratio. Any one of four ratios might have been logically employed; (1) the ratio of pleasant to unpleasant memories; (2) its inversion, unpleasant to pleasant memories; (3) the ratio of pleasant memories to the total number of memories; (4) the ratio of unpleasant memories to the total number. Since the first two of these are inversely proportional, they are equivalent to one another for comparative purposes. Because some neutral memories are included in the total number, the last two ratios are not true inverse proportions, but they approximate this relationship since the number of neutral memories was small. Consequently, the number of choices is reduced to two: one of the former ratios or one of the latter ratios. It was decided to use the latter ratios because the denominator in them is larger, being equal to the total number of memories. Since a score derived from a ratio is an index score, the advantage of a large denominator is that the index fluctuates less with changes in the numerator. There is a tendency for index scores to introduce a degree of spuriousness into comparisons, but this is diminished by a large denominator. In addition, by making comparisons only of the extremes the spuriousness is reduced to a minimum.

The ratio finally adopted to express the relative frequency of pleasant and unpleasant memories was the number of unpleasant memories divided by the total, which may be expressed by the formula, U/T. Table XIII shows the mean, the standard deviation, and the range of the quotients that were obtained by the use of this formula for both male and female subjects. Combined recall scores of the first and second periods were used as a basis for calculation.

TABLE XIII
MEAN, STANDARD DEVIATION, AND RANGE OF U/T SCORES

	Mean	S.D.	Range
Male ($N=48$)	31.82	10.44	8–51
Female ($N=76$)	32.54	9.35	10–54

Very little difference between sexes is observed. This might have been anticipated by the preceding findings on the similarity between the sexes. Again the variation among individuals is appreciable. If these scores are reliable there is justification for comparing them with the results of the various psychological tests which the subjects were given. As in the

TABLE XIV
RELIABILITY COEFFICIENTS OF U/T SCORES

	r	P.E.$_r$
Male	.64	.057
Female	.57	.052

case of the recall scores (see page 9) reliability was estimated by correlating the U/T score of the first recall period with the U/T score of the second period. The results of these correlations are presented in Table XIV. While these coefficients are not high, they do have predictive value at the extremes, which is all that was required for purposes of the present study.

The subjects were divided into quartiles on the basis of their U/T scores. In Table XV the subjects with high, low, and average U/T scores are compared in regard to their results on the five psychological tests. A high score in this case indicates a relatively higher degree of retention of *unpleasant* experiences. Subjects with high U/T scores are those that would be described in the terminology that has developed as *memory pessimists*. A low U/T score, on the other hand, would indicate a memory optimist.

Again very little difference in the psychological test scores of the three groups was detected. The significance of the differences between the extremes was tested by dividing the differences by their standard error. These results are presented in Table XVI. Although the difference between the mean U/T scores of the high and low groups (memory pessimists and optimists) is very reliable for both sexes, in only one other instance is there any indication of a significant difference. This is in the case of the male scores on the Thurstone Personality Schedule. The males with the higher

TABLE XV
A COMPARISON OF TEST RESULTS OF INDIVIDUALS WITH
HIGH, AVERAGE, AND LOW U/T SCORES

	Mean Scores		
	Upper 25%	Middle 50%	Lower 25%
U/T Score			
Male	46.00	32.43	18.92
Female	44.06	33.18	19.61
Intelligence			
Male	56.25	57.78	63.15
Female	50.22	52.79	49.61
Memory			
Male	24.27	25.13	29.17
Female	25.24	22.62	24.56
Emotional Stability			
Male	60.83	33.67	33.92
Female	46.33	39.33	41.39
Ascendance-Submission			
Male	52.66	50.86	48.92
Female	51.22	55.63	55.39
Conservatism-Radicalism			
Male	62.09	54.76	58.31
Female	50.89	51.90	48.00

TABLE XVI

SIGNIFICANCE OF THE DIFFERENCES IN TEST RESULTS BETWEEN INDIVIDUALS WITH HIGH AND LOW U/T SCORES

Test	Difference Between Means	Difference / σ Diff.
U/T Scores		
Male	26.08	12.42
Female	24.45	14.91
Intelligence		
Male	6.90	0.55
Female	0.61	0.21
Memory		
Male	4.90	1.78
Female	0.68	0.38
Emotional Stability		
Male	26.91	2.95
Female	4.94	0.75
Ascendance-Submission		
Male	3.74	0.61
Female	4.17	1.00
Conservatism-Radicalism		
Male	3.78	0.64
Female	2.89	0.67

U/T scores (memory pessimists) have a higher average score on the Thurstone Personality Schedule than do those with the low U/T scores (memory optimists) indicating a higher degree of emotional instability or neurotic tendency for the former group. The difference between the average Thurstone scores of these two groups divided by its standard error is 2.95. It is of interest to note that the average Thurstone score of the middle fifty percent is almost identical with that of the lower twenty-five percent indicating that the relationship between U/T scores and Thurstone scores exists only at the upper end of the distribution. This suggests that individuals, at least males, who remember relatively more unpleasant events from their childhood have a greater degree of neurotic tendency. Such a generalization, if it could be established, has many provocative ramifications, but without additional evidence it can only be regarded as an interesting possibility.

Just as in the case of the total recall scores, the results, though inconclusive, suggest the possibility that non-intellective traits of personality play a determining role in the selection of childhood memories. Again the limitations of the questionnaire method for adequately diagnosing personality factors relevant to childhood recall should be emphasized.

SOME THEORETICAL CONSIDERATIONS

"Dependence upon the past (*mneme*)," says Stern (39, p. 189) "is a fundamental principle of all organic life." One cannot disagree with this assertion, nor can one question the adaptive function of memory. In memory the experiences of the past are conserved and made available for the immediate adjustive requirements of the organism, and in this very direct way memory serves the basic needs of the organism. It should be expected, then, that the needs of the organism (drives, attitudes, interests, sentiments, and wishes) should condition, influence and direct mnemonic activity just as they influence and direct other activities of the organism. Further since individuals have different constellations of needs, it follows that the effect of these needs on the mnemonic functions will vary from one person to the next. What is relevant for one individual may not be relevant for another; and what is relevant on one occasion may be irrelevant on the next.[32] This was strikingly demonstrated in the present study when approximately fifty percent of the memories reported during the second recall period were new, despite the fact that the subjects presumably had the same associative set dur-

---

[32] Pear (31) distinguishes between logical and affective relevance. The comments above refer particularly to the latter.

ing both recall periods. The early work of Colegrove (8) is of the utmost pertinence in this connection. Although his results were not systematically presented and cannot be accepted as conclusive, they are, nevertheless, extremely suggestive. He apparently obtained evidence, through questioning individuals of different age groups, that the content of childhood memories varied with age. For example, adolescent males reported more motor memories, while males in their thirties reported more memories involving reflection and thought. The implication is that the mnemonic selective factors were influenced by the total life pattern of the individual and reflected changing interests and attitudes.

Thus it is believed that the experiences recalled by the subjects of the present study were of personal relevance, and, despite the fact that no relationship was found between them and the psychological measures employed, it is felt that these memories were related to the personality structures of the subjects and to their needs and feelings. If such a relationship did exist, apparently a more intimate and dynamic analysis than is possible through the use of paper and pencil tests was needed to discover it. This is a question which could probably be explored with much profit and certainly warrants further investigation.

There is good reason to believe that the variations that were noted among the subjects in regard to the affect of their memories are especially significant. It has already been stated that there was no way of knowing the extent to which such variations were influenced by differences in original childhood experience, but there is plenty of evidence from other sources that most people tend to forget the disagreeable or the unpleasant. This same tendency was apparent in the present investigation. Obliviscence of the disagreeable, then, seems to be the general tendency. There is much variation in this tendency, however, and with some persons it is reversed. Most persons, in other words, best express their needs through memory by retaining what is agreeable and expelling what is disagreeable, while a few react in an opposite fashion. The affective tone of associations is thus seen to serve as either an excitatory or inhibitory influence on their emergence into consciousness. This seems to be true whether the affective tone is either pleasant or unpleasant.

The theory of repression has accustomed us to think in terms of the avoidance of painful associations. However, the adaptive significance of retaining disagreeable or painful memories should not be overlooked, as one is apt to do through too literal an interpretation of the *pleasure principle.* Certainly this is not intended by the Freudian or any other theory of psychological hedonism which recognizes that the recall of painful experiences of the past permits one to make less painful and more adaptive adjustments in the future. In fact, it is the inability to recall certain experiences which is generally regarded as the basis of hysterical, phobic and other neurotic symptoms, which presumably may be alleviated through the recollection of these same experiences.

In metaphorical terms one might thus speak of the "seeking of pain" through memory as well as of the "seeking of pleasure." Thus conceived, there are two interacting and opposing mnemonic tendencies which function in the interests of organismic adjustment. One might expect that where the individual is making an adequate adjustment, some sort of harmonious balance between these two tendencies would be effected. On the other hand, an exaggeration of either tendency with a corresponding inhibition of the other might be a concomitant of maladjustment. In other words either the extreme memory-optimist or the extreme memory-pessimist might be inhibiting a fundamental mnemonic tendency at the cost of balanced adjustment. Further, it would be reasonable to expect that memory-optimism and memory-pessimism would be related to other traits of personality, including choice of symptoms, where psychopathology is present.

As evidence of this Rosenzweig (34) has recently presented experimental evidence to show that some persons remember successes better than failures, while others reverse this tendency. He suggests that, whereas repression (of painful experiences) is a preferred mode of defense with the former individuals, with the latter it is not. Further, Rosenzweig and Sarason (35) have shown that repression as a preferred mode of defense is associated with hypnotizability as a personality trait and with impunitiveness as a characteristic immediate reaction to frustration. On the contrary, those individuals who do not employ repression as a defense mechanism are characteristically extra-punitive and non-hypnotizable. While memory for successes and failures cannot be considered identical with memory for pleasant and unpleasant events, a possible relationship is suggested of which further investigation is certainly warranted.

SUGGESTIONS FOR FUTURE RESEARCH

From the results of the present study, it is apparent that the most pressing need is for surveys of childhood memories in which the subjects would be studied intensively so as to permit an intimate and detailed personality analysis of each. The memories could then be regarded as *themas* and studied in the context of the whole personality. Attempts at this have been briefly reported by Adler (1) and Murray et al. (30). More work, however, needs to be done along these lines. An intensive personal analysis would permit a consideration of the extent to which distortion of childhood memories occurs and perhaps a determination of the incidence of screen memories.

More information is needed on the differences among various age groups in their ability to recall childhood events. The theory of infantile amnesia implies that childhood recall would not vary much with age. A comparison of pre-adolescents, adolescents, and adults of various ages might supply critical data in this regard.

A comparison of individuals more widely dispersed in intelligence than was true of the subjects of the present study would also be desirable.

It would be interesting to collect memories beyond the age of eight. A comparison of memories of different life periods, e.g., childhood memories with those of adolescence might yield valuable data.

Although the problem does not specifically relate to childhood memory, more work should be done on the dynamics of memory-optimism and memory-pessimism and on personality differences between memory-optimists and memory-pessimists.

IV. Summary

THE FOREGOING investigation was designed to study individual differences among college students in their ability to recall childhood experiences. Differences in both the frequency and affective character of memories from the first eight years of life were studied. Further, an attempt was made to relate these differences to various psychological traits—both intellective and non-intellective.

The subjects, numbering 48 males and 76 females, recorded their memories during two recall periods lasting 85 minutes each and separated by an interval ranging from 35 to 40 days. The second recall period, which was not announced in advance, was used as a check on the first, and the instructions for both periods were identical.

While wide individual variations in the number of memories were noted among the subjects, it was found that the averages for males and females were remarkably similar, indicating very little, if any, sex differences in this respect. In order to determine individual consistency, the number of memories of each subject for the first recall period was correlated with the number of each for the second period. The coefficients were found to be .70 for the males and .76 for the females. It was felt that these coefficients were sufficiently high to warrant the conclusion that individual differences in the ability to recall childhood events are not of a purely haphazard nature, some persons being able to recall consistently more of their childhood experiences than others.

A comparison of the memories for each of the two periods showed that an average of almost 50 percent of those recorded during the second period had not been recorded previously. Hence a total recall score was obtained by adding the new memories of the second period to the total of the first period. When this was done the average combined total was roughly 51 memories for males and 53 memories for females.

When the memories were plotted according to the age of their origin, it was found that there was an increment from year to year which took the form of an ogive and seemed to parallel the growth of language and memory during childhood. This suggested, first, that memory for childhood events might be related to the level of mental development at the time of their occurrence; and, second, that factors besides repression determine the extent and content of childhood recollections. Indeed the relatively large number of memories from the early years (elicited under far from ideal conditions) and their gradual increase with age stand in apparent contradiction to the Freudian doctrines of infantile amnesia.

When the memories were studied in terms of their affect, it was found that the emotions which the subjects recalled as having prevailed at the time of the original experiences were numerous and varied. Most commonly experienced was *joy*, which constituted about 30 percent of the total. Next in frequency was *fear*, about 15 percent, followed by *pleasure, anger, grief,* and *excitement,* all between 5 and 10 percent. Only very slight differences were noted between male and female subjects. The great variety and intensity of emotion accompanying these early experiences challenges the contention that childhood memories are for the most part banal screen-memories.

Recall of pleasant events was more frequent than unpleasant or neutral events. In round numbers, pleasant memories constituted about 50 percent of the total, unpleasant memories about 30 percent, and neutral memories about 20 percent. While pleasant memories predominated with most subjects, some reversed this trend; and it was suggested that the terms, *memory-optimist* and *memory-pessimist,* used by other investigators, might also apply in this instance. The ratio of the number of unpleasant memories to the total number of memories (U/T) was used as an index of the degree of optimism-pessimism. That this trait was reasonably consistent was demonstrated by correlating the U/T ratios of the first and second recall periods. The coefficients obtained were .64 for the males and .57 for the females. It is also interesting to note that while there was a gradual increase of the number of experiences recalled with age, the relative incidence of pleasant, unpleasant, and neutral memories remained quite constant from year to year.

Individual differences in the frequency of recall and the degree of optimism-pessimism were both studied in relation to the following traits: general intelligence, memory, emotional stability, ascendance-submission, and radicalism-conservatism. The results of these comparisons were essentially inconclusive. However, it was felt that the lack of observed relationship between psychological traits and childhood memory could easily have been due to the limitations of the measuring devices employed, and were not necessarily indicative of the absence of such a relationship.

Certain theoretical implications of the results were discussed, and suggestions for future research were made.

V. Appendix

A. PRELIMINARY STATEMENT TO SUBJECTS

When each group was first assembled, the following statement was spoken to the subjects in a natural manner:

Although probably none of you has ever before served as a subject for an experiment, I am sure that you all know enough about experiments to realize that all relevant factors must be as carefully controlled as possible. In experiments in physics or chemistry this is a comparatively simple matter, but in psychology, where highly complicated human subject must be used, it is a matter of the utmost difficulty. Indeed, it is impossible to do, unless the experimenter can secure the wholehearted cooperation of his subjects. For regardless of how carefully the experimenter lays his plans, regardless of how scrupulously he executes them, or how painstakingly he analyzes his results, they are of little value if his subjects have not contributed their sincerest efforts.

I know that students joke about being guinea pigs, but actually you will play a much more active part than guinea pigs ever can. Guinea pigs are *used* to conduct experiments. Human subjects are *asked to cooperate* in them. I remind you of these things in order that you may fully appreciate your role as subject, which is as important as that of the experimenter.

You are aware that this series of experiments will last through several sessions, and will contain many parts. At all times be sure that you understand the directions and then follow them carefully. This is all I will say; the rest I leave up to you.

B. FORM FOR RECORDING MEMORIES

The form with which the subjects were provided was made from fourteen by seventeen inch foolscap, horizontally lined. Vertical lines were drawn to provide spaces for:

(1) Numbering the memories.
(2) Recording them.
(3) Checking the certainty with which they were recalled.
(4) Recording their age.
(5) Indicating their affective character.
(6) Stating the accompanying emotions.

The vertical lines were drawn in red and blue to aid the subjects in distinguishing the columns.

C. INSTRUCTIONS FOR RECORDING CHILDHOOD EXPERIENCES

The following instructions for recording their childhood experiences were given to the subjects. They were spoken slowly and in a natural manner. After they were completed, the salient points were written on the blackboard in outline form to provide a reference for the subjects who were then given an opportunity to ask questions regarding them.

The form which you have just been given is to be used to record the early experiences of your life. You are to include experiences up to your eighth birthday. This was approximately the time that most of you started the third grade. I want you to record all the experiences which you are able to remember as well as those which you yourself cannot recall, but that have been told to you.

Number each experience in the extreme left hand column which is marked NO. Your memories as well as experiences which you personally do not remember are to be recorded in the space marked MEMORY. In reporting these try to include only a single experience at a time, describing it briefly without omitting any essential details. After you have written an experience, indicate whether you remember it, do not remember it, or are in doubt about remembering it by placing a check in one of the next three columns, marked REM for remember, DON'T REM for do not remember, and DOUBT for doubtful. Following this indicate the age of each experience, as nearly as you can estimate it, in the column marked AGE. For example, if you were four years old at the time of a given experience you would place a 4 in the column. Thus, no experience will be marked higher than 7 since only those experiences occurring before your eighth birthday are to be included. In case you include any before you were one year old, estimate your age in terms of months. To assist you in recalling the age of your experiences, use as points of reference outstanding events, such as moving, starting school, illness or accidents, birth or death of relatives, trips and vacations, or any others that you can locate fairly accurately.

After you have recorded its age draw a line under the experience extending it all the way across the page and go on to the next one. If memories do not come at once do not give up but continue to concentrate on this early period. It is surprising sometimes how new recollections will appear when we think we have exhausted our store of them. You will have about an hour and a half in which to write.

After eighty-five minutes the subjects were instructed as follows:

The time for recording is up, will you now go over your childhood experiences one by one and indicate by a check in the appropriate column whether each was very pleasant, pleasant, neutral, unpleasant, or very unpleasant. Use the six narrow columns labeled AFF for this purpose. VP stands for *very pleasant*, P for *pleasant*, N for *neutral*, U for *unpleasant*, and VU for *very unpleasant*. If an experience was both pleasant and unpleasant, you should place a check in two columns. Try to remember how you felt *at the time* of the experience. If you cannot remember, place a check in the column marked CR. At the same time you are to write any emotions that accompanied the experience in the column marked EM. I will not give you a list of emotional terms. You select the terms that seem most appropriate in each case. Be sure to record your feelings and emotions at the time of the original experience.

When the subjects appeared for the second recall session (thirty-five to forty days later) the instructions were repeated verbatim except that at the end of the first paragraph of instructions the following statement was inserted:

Focus your attention on your childhood and not on what you may have written the last time you recorded your childhood experiences. Whether or not an experience was included last time is immaterial. The only thing that matters is that it occurred during the first eight years.

D. THE MEYER MEMORY TEST

This battery, which has not been published, was constructed by Professor George Meyer, formerly of the Psychology Department of the University of Michigan. An abridged form suitable for use in the present experiment, was employed. It included the following tests:

(1) Memory for digits (forward).
(2) Memory for words.
(3) Memory for sentences.
(4) Memory for story (reconstruction).
(5) Memory for story (questions and answers).

For *digits* and *words* there were two items at each level of difficulty. If either item was correct, the level was regarded as successfully passed. The score was the number of digits or words at the last level of success preceding two successive failures. For *sentences* the same criterion of success was used. The score was the number of syllables at the upper level of success.

The score for the *reconstruction story*, was the number of ideas correctly reproduced; while for the *question and answer story*, the score was the number of correct answers.

The individual test scores were equally weighted by converting them into standard scores, and these were added together to give the final total score.

E. CRITERIA FOR DETERMINING A SINGLE EXPERIENCE

As stated on page 7 the criteria for a single experience were temporal continuity and/or contextual unity. That is, two items were regarded as constituting only one if they were joined together in time or were related in context. Usually both factors existed simultaneously. Conversely, a single item would be subdivided if it contained disparate elements. This can best be illustrated by examples. Following are several examples of separate items that were combined:

1a. Neil (brother) goes to school—kindergarden.
1b. I miss Neil and want to go to school.
2a. My first pair of glasses.
2b. The day that I received my glasses mother took me to show.
3a. My mother went away. So I had to stay home from school to stay with Frances (visiting cousin) who was afraid to remain home alone.
3b. I wanted to go to school instead of remaining with Frances. So I ran away from home and went to school. My big brother who was a traffic boy came to find me in my classroom.

Following are examples of single items that were subdivided:

1a. My grandfather died on Memorial Day; my mother cried, and I thought she was laughing.
1b. The next day I had chicken pox and I couldn't go to the funeral.
2a. I had two cats when I was very small. Tabby Grey (I named it) was a female. Once she had two kittens, a white one and a black one. When they were very tiny some big boys stoned them and I found their bodies. I felt very bad since they were my only playmates.
2b. Once I took the other cat to my grandmother's in Algonac for a ride. The cat killed one of her baby chickens and I got an awful scolding.

F. FREQUENCY OF EMOTIONAL TERMS

Male

Affection 4	Abashed 1	Curiosity 44
Adventurous 5	Aesthetic 1	Crowded 1
Admiration 5		Calmness 1
Awkward 1	Blush 1	Conquest 1
Amazed 14	Beauty 1	Congeniality 1
Abused 1	Beligerent 1	Condemnation 1
Amusing 7	Boredom 6	Comfortable 1
Average 1	Boldness 1	Complacency 1
Anger 133	Bewilderment 6	Confinement 1
Ambition 1	Bad 2	Conceited 1
Anticipation 3	Being wronged 2	Cocky 4
Alarm 1		Conscious-stricken 1
Awe 12	Cool 1	
Afraid 12	Cheat 1	Dislike 21
Anxiety 23	Cry 2	Discouraged 1
Astonishment 3	Contentment 23	Dread 3
Annoyed 2	Critical 1	Doubt 1

Disappointment	26	
Devilish	7	
Depression	6	
Discomfort	5	
Downhearted	1	
Disapproval	1	
Dissatisfaction	1	
Desire	4	
Displeasure	3	
Dejection	1	
Disgust	30	
Distaste	1	
Delighted	20	
Dull	2	
Dumb	1	
Determination	2	
Desperation	2	
Despair	1	
Desire (to swim)	1	
Desire (to read)	1	
Expectancy	8	
Envy	7	
Eager	2	
Enjoyment	41	
Elated	18	
Excitement	127	
Eventful	1	
Embarrassment	28	
Equality	1	
Enthused	1	
Fear	441	
Felt important	3	
Free	2	
Frightened	25	
Fun	85	
Familiarity	1	
Fear of death	1	
Felt badly	2	
Friendship	3	
Foolish	1	
Forced	1	
Fascination	8	
Funny	3	
Friendliness	2	
Frustration	9	
Felt strange	1	
Felt sorry	1	
Fatigue	1	
Glad	4	
Guilt	6	
Grown up	3	
Gloom	10	
Grief	34	
Grief-stricken	1	
Great	1	
Griped	1	
Good	3	
Good time	3	
Greedy	1	
Gay	1	
Happiness	276	
Heartbroken	1	
Humiliation	8	
Hunger	1	

Helpless	6	
Hope	1	
Hurt	18	
Had to have way	1	
Hysterical	1	
Helpful	1	
Horrible	1	
Hate	51	
Headaches	1	
Horror	2	
Hardship	1	
Humor	2	
Inferiority	2	
Interest	82	
Irritability	1	
Impatient	4	
Independence	1	
Inquisitiveness	2	
Illness	2	
Insecurity	1	
Jealousy	7	
Joy	526	
Jolly	1	
Love	98	
Laughter	1	
Lucky	1	
Liked	6	
Loyalty	1	
Longing	2	
Lonelines	7	
Laziness	1	
Loss	1	
Lust	2	
Like a dope	1	
Mischievous	2	
Mixed up	2	
Mad	15	
Meanness	1	
Mortification	1	
Melancholy	1	
Miserable	2	
Not understanding	1	
Nuts	3	
Nausea	3	
Numbness	1	
Nastiness	1	
Nice	2	
Nostalgia	1	
Offended	1	
Outraged	1	
Obstinate	2	
Oppression	4	
O. K.	1	
Proud	33	
Peacefulness	3	
Pain	53	
Pleasant	63	
Passive	4	
Pride	36	
Petty-love	1	
Pity	11	

Pleased	3	
Pleasure	212	
Puzzled	5	
Punished	1	
Puppy love	1	
Queer	1	
Rage	6	
Revulsion	1	
Remorsefulness	5	
Relief	5	
Repulsion	1	
Resentment	3	
Repent	1	
Revenge	2	
Restless	2	
Rebellion	3	
Ridiculous	1	
Rejected	1	
Revolt	1	
Retribution	1	
Regret	5	
Rapture	2	
Sympathy	1	
Surprise	37	
Strangeness	1	
Sorrow	62	
Shame	36	
Scheming	1	
Sadness	50	
Shocked	1	
Safe	1	
Sorry	7	
Success	2	
Superior	3	
Swell	5	
Sickening	2	
Security	3	
Satisfaction	24	
Serenity	1	
Stubborness	2	
Suspense	1	
Suffocating	1	
Sick	7	
Self-pity	2	
Self-satisfaction	2	
Scared	24	
Selfishness	1	
Strength	1	
Smart	3	
Sleepy	1	
Self-confident	1	
Self-conscious	4	
Soothing	1	
Stunned	1	
Scorned	1	
Startled	1	
Sheepish	1	
Shyness	5	
Stage Fright	2	
Thrill of accomplishment	1	
Thrill of talking	1	
Tiring	1	
Tiresome	1	
Terror	2	

Thrill 20	Unlucky 1	Unfamiliar 2
Thrill of competition 1	Unfairness 1	
Thwarted 1	Unhappy 15	Weakness 1
Tiredness 1	Unwanted 1	Wonder 39
Temper 1	Uneasiness 2	Worry 5
Terrible 1	Uncertainty 8	Wrong doing 1
Timid 1	Unpleasant 15	Wonderful 1

Female

Accomplishment 4	Competition 2	Enthused 2
Awful 2	Confusion 6	Effort 1
Acceptance 1	Caution 1	Exhaustion 1
Acting mature 1	Conflict 1	Entertaining 15
Affection 5	Contempt 1	Exasperation 1
Adventurous 8	Consideration 1	Empty 1
Admiration 4	Concern 1	Empathy 1
Amazed 10	Compassion 1	
Amusing 23		Fear 610
Anger 258	Dislike 28	Free 1
Ambition 3	Dread 6	Frightened 64
Anticipation 19	Doubt 1	Fun 248
Alarm 2	Disappointment 75	Foolish 2
Awe 40	Devilish 1	Fascination 12
Afraid 21	Depression 4	Funny 9
Anxiety 19	Discomfort 19	Friendliness 2
Astonishment 2	Dissatisfaction 1	Frustration 2
Annoyed 24	Desire 6	Fatigue 2
Approval 1	Displeasure 1	Fiendish joy 1
Appreciation 1	Distrust 4	Fondness 1
Agitated 1	Didn't mind 1	Failure 1
Absorption 1	Desire for attention 2	Flattered 1
Attractiveness 2	Distress 1	Felt sorry 1
Achievement 4	Dominance 1	
Adoration 2	Discontent 1	Glad 29
Aggravating 1	Daring 1	Guilt 6
Aloneness 1	Disagreeable 2	Grown up 5
Apprehension 4	Defiant 2	Gloom 11
Anger at self 1	Didn't belong 1	Grief 107
Attention 1	Disinterest 2	Good 4
Astounded 1	Desire to be left alone ... 1	Good time 1
	Disrespect 1	Greedy 5
Brave 1	Dejection 2	Gay 11
Beauty 2	Disgust 53	Gratefulness 5
Boredom 19	Distaste 11	Glee 10
Bewilderment 24	Delighted 32	Good will 1
Bad 1	Dull 2	
Bliss 1	Determination 2	Happiness 303
Backward 1	Despair 3	Humiliation 22
Benevolence 1	Disturbing 1	Hunger 1
Bad feelings 1	Disillusioned 1	Helpless 1
Bad taste 1	Dreariness 1	Hope 2
Baffled 1	Disbelief 2	Hurt 26
Bashful 1	Different 2	Haunted me 1
	Deceit 2	Hesitant 1
Capable 1	Desire to accomplish 1	Hurt myself 1
Cooped up 1	Didn't care 1	Hysterical 2
Cry 1		Helpful 2
Contentment 27	Exultation 1	Horrible 3
Curiosity 113	Expectancy 7	Hate 61
Calmness 1	Envy 9	Horror 14
Condemnation 1	Eager 6	Humor 1
Comfortable 3	Enjoyment 80	Hurt feelings 2
Cruelty 1	Elated 19	
Companionship 3	Excitement 285	Intellectual maturity 1
Chastised 2	Eventful 1	Inferiority 4
Comical 3	Embarrassment 71	Interest 78

Irritability	4	
Impatient	5	
Independence	3	
Illness	2	
Insecurity	3	
Imagination	2	
Injustice	1	
Importance	5	
Indignation	3	
Insignificance	1	
Jealousy	21	
Joy	993	
Jolly	2	
Just a memory	1	
Kindness	1	
Longing for someone	1	
Love	45	
Laughter	1	
Liked	14	
Loneliness	10	
Lust	1	
Loathing	2	
Lack of enthusiasm	1	
Lethargy	1	
Lack of understanding	1	
Leisure	1	
Lack of security	3	
Lack of interest	1	
Mischievous	3	
Mad	21	
Meanness	4	
Melancholy	3	
Miserable	9	
Misunderstanding	1	
Mature	3	
Mysterious	5	
Martyred	1	
Moody	1	
Merry	1	
Mild	1	
Nonchalance	2	
Nice	2	
Nervous	10	
Neglected	2	
Normal	1	
Nice feeling	1	
Nerve wracked	1	
New	3	
No self-respect	1	
Naughtiness	1	
Outraged	1	
Obedient	1	
Overjoyed	2	

Play	3	
Proud	24	
Peacefulness	1	
Pain	84	
Pleasant	27	
Physical upset	1	
Pugnacious	1	
Perplexing	1	
Panic	3	
Progress	1	
Peeved	2	
Passive	4	
Pride	194	
Pity	16	
Pleased	18	
Pleasure	244	
Puzzled	5	
Puppy love	2	
Peculiar	1	
Question morals	1	
Questioning	1	
Revulsion	1	
Routine	2	
Remorsefulness	8	
Relief	4	
Resentment	8	
Repent	2	
Revenge	5	
Restless	1	
Rebellion	1	
Regret	3	
Respect	2	
Relent	1	
Responsibility	1	
Reluctance	2	
Release	1	
Restriction	1	
Sober	1	
Sympathy	4	
Surprise	65	
Strangeness	6	
Shame	74	
Sorrow	91	
Sadness	119	
Shocked	7	
Sorry	6	
Success	1	
Superior	5	
Security	6	
Satisfaction	18	
Stubbornness	6	
Sick	6	
Self-pity	5	
Self-satisfaction	5	
Scared	36	
Selfishness	3	
Smart	2	

Sleepy	2	
Self-conscious	2	
Sorry	1	
Self-gratification	1	
Sorry for myself	1	
Suspicion	1	
Silliness	2	
Solitude	1	
Self-importance	1	
Save money	1	
Solemnity	1	
Spitefulness	2	
Self-disgust	1	
Sweet tooth	1	
Sophistication	1	
Smugness	1	
Self-centered	1	
Serious	1	
Shyness	3	
Triumph	7	
Tiresome	1	
Terror	20	
Thrill	41	
Tiredness	1	
Temper	1	
Timid	2	
Teasing	2	
Thoughtfulness	2	
Thought him silly	1	
Troublesome	1	
Tearful	1	
Unhappy	32	
Uneasiness	1	
Uncertainty	5	
Unpleasant	16	
Understanding	1	
Unexpectant	1	
Unconcern	6	
Uncomfortable	4	
Upset	1	
Unknown element	1	
Unsocial	1	
Unexplained	1	
Vanity	1	
Wonder	40	
Worry	5	
Wistfulness	1	
Wept	1	
Warmth	1	
Wisdom	1	
Worship	1	
Wanting explanation	1	
Weary	1	
Well-being	1	
Yearning	1	

BIBLIOGRAPHY

1. ADLER, A. Erste Kindheitserinnerungen. *Int. Z. Indiv.-Psychol.*, 1933, *11*, 81-90.
2. ALLPORT, G. W. *Personality. A psychological interpretation.* New York: Henry Holt, 1937.
3. BELL, S. A preliminary study of the emotions of love between the sexes. *Amer. J. Psychol.*, 1902, *13*, 325-354.
4. BLONSKY, P. Das Problem der ersten Kindheitserinnerung und seine Bedeutung. *Arch. ges. Psychol.*, 1929, *71*, 369-390.
5. BRIDGES, K. M. B. Emotional development in early infancy. *Child Develpm.*, 1932, *3*, 324-341.
6. BROWN, J. F. *The psychodynamics of abnormal behavior.* New York: McGraw-Hill, 1940.
7. CHILD, I. L. The relation between measures of infantile amnesia and of neuroticism. *J. abnorm. soc. Psychol.*, 1940, *35*, 453-456.
8. COLEGROVE, F. W. Individual memories. *Amer. J. Psychol.*, 1899, *10*, 228-255.
9. CROOK, M. N. AND HARDEN, L. A quantitative investigation of early memories. *J. soc. Psychol.*, 1931, 2, 252-255.
10. DUDYCHA, G. J. An objective study of punctuality in relation to personality and achievement. *Arch. Psychol., N.Y.*, 1936, No. 204.
11. DUDYCHA, G. J. AND DUDYCHA, M. M. Childhood memories: a review of the literature. *Psychol. Bull.*, 1941, *38*, 668-682.
12. DUDYCHA, G. J. AND DUDYCHA, M. M. Adolescents' memories of preschool experiences. *J. genet. Psychol.*, 1933, *42*, 468-480.
13. DUDYCHA, G. J. AND DUDYCHA, M. M. Some factors and characteristics in childhood memories. *Child Develpm.*, 1933, *4*, 265-278.
14. FREUD, S. *A general introduction to psychoanalysis.* New York: Garden City Publishing Co., 1938.
15. FREUD, S. The unconscious. In *Collected Papers.* London: Hogarth Press, 1925. Vol. IV.
16. FREUD, S. Three contributions to the theory of sex. In *The basic writings of Sigmund Freud* (Ed. A. A. Brill). New York: Modern Library, 1938.
17. GOODENOUGH, F. L. The measurement of mental growth. In *A handbook of child psychology*, Rev. Ed., (Ed. Carl Murchison). Worcester: Clark Univ. Press, 1933.
18. GORDON, K. A study of early memories. *J. Delinqu.*, 1928, *12*, 129-132.
19. HADFIELD, J. A. The reliability of infantile memories. *Brit. J. med. Psychol.*, 1928, *8*, 87-111.
20. HALL, G. S. Note on early memories. *Ped. Sem.*, 1899, *6*, 485-512.
21. HEINEMANN, E. Das erste Schuljahr in der Erinnerung des Erwachsenen. *Z. Kinderforsch.*, 1939, *48*, 22-71.
22. HENDERSON, E. N. Do we forget the disagreeable? *J. Phil. Psychol. sci. Meth.*, 1911, *8*, 432-438.
23. HENNIG, R. Die Zahl der datierbaren Erinnerungen eines Menschenlebens. *Z. Psychol.*, 1937, *140*, 330-356.
24. HENRI, V. AND HENRI, C. Earliest recollections. *Pop. Sci. Mon.*, 1898, *53*, 108-115.
25. JERSILD, A. T. Memory for the pleasant as compared with the unpleasant. *J. Exp. Psychol.*, 1931, *14*, 284-288.
26. JERSILD, A. T. AND HOLMES, F. B. Children's fears. *Child Develpm. Monogr.*, No. 20.
27. MEANS, M. H. Fears of one thousand college women. *J. Abnorm. soc. Psychol.*, 1936, *31*, 291-311.
28. MELTZER, H. Individual differences in forgetting pleasant and unpleasant experiences. *J. Educ. Psychol.*, 1930, *21*, 399-409.
29. MILES, C. A study of individual psychology. *Amer. J. Psychol.*, 1893, *6*, 534-558.
30. MURRAY, H. A. et al. *Explorations in personality.* New York: Oxford Univ. Press, 1938.
31. PEAR, T. H. *Remembering and forgetting.* New York: Dutton, 1922.
32. POTWIN, E. B. Study of early memories. *Psychol. Rev.*, 1901, *8*, 596-601.
33. RAPAPORT, D. *Emotions and memory.* Baltimore: Williams and Wilkins, 1942.
34. ROSENZWEIG, S. An experimental study of repression with special reference to need-persistive and ego-defensive reactions to frustration. *J. exp. Psychol.*, 1943, *32*, 64-74.
35. ROSENZWEIG, S. AND SARASON, S. An experimental study of the triadic hypothesis: reaction to frustration, ego-defense, and hypnotizability. *Character and Pers.*, 1942, *11*, 1-19; 150-165.
36. SEARS, R. R. Functional abnormalities of memory with special reference to amnesia. *Psychol. Bull.*, 1936, *33*, 229-274.
37. SHELDON, W. H. AND STEVENS, S. S. *The varieties of temperament.* New York: Harper and Brothers.
38. SMITH, M. E. An investigation of the development of the sentence and the extent of vocabulary in young children. *University of Iowa Studies: Studies in child welfare.* Iowa City: University of Iowa Press, 1926, Vol. 3, No. 5.
39. STERN, WILLIAM. *General psychology.* New York: Macmillan, 1938.
40. THURSTONE, L. L. AND ACKERSON, L. The mental growth curve for the Binet tests. *J. Educ. Psychol.*, 1929, *20*, 569-583.
41. WINCH, W. H. *Children's perceptions.* Baltimore: Warwick and Yorke, 1914.
42. WOHLGEMUTH, A. The influence of feeling on memory. *Brit. J. Psychol.*, 1923, *13*, 405-416.

150.8
P974
v. 62
no. 4
  Psychological monographs:
general and applied -
The frequency and affective
character of childhood

150.8
P974
v. 62
no. 4
  Psychological monographs:
general and applied - The
frequency and affective character
of childhood memories, by Samuel
Waldfogel

CPSIA information can be obtained
at www.ICGtesting.com
Printed in the USA
BVHW090813070119
537207BV00021B/2337/P